THE SOUTHEAST ASIAN WORLD

BY THE SAME AUTHOR

The Chinese People & the Chinese Earth

THE SOUTHEAST ASIAN WORLD

An Introductory Essay

KEITH BUCHANAN
Professor of Geography, Victoria University of Wellington
Wellington, New Zealand

LONDON: G. BELL AND SONS, LTD

G. BELL AND SONS, LTD
York House, Portugal Street
London, W.C.2

Printed in Great Britain by
The Camelot Press Ltd., London and Southampton

À

Son Altesse

Contents

Maps and Cartograms

Plates

Between pages 80 and 81

(7, 9, 10 & 42 from photographs by Iain Buchanan; other photographs by the author)

Foreword

THIS VOLUME has two objectives: first, to provide a general introduction to an understanding of the Southeast Asian world, of its peoples, their problems and their aspirations; secondly, to provide a general background to the more specialised regional and systematic studies which are projected in this series. Its viewpoint is basically geographical, although in writing it I have been little concerned with the conventional 'frontiers' of the subject. Indeed, to attain an understanding of an area such as Southeast Asia it is often necessary to reject the cramped confines of the single discipline and draw extensively on related disciplines—in this case, history, sociology and economics. The volume is not primarily concerned with description, rather is it concerned with trends, with the forces that have shaped and are continuing to shape the turbulent and diverse nations of the region. Such an emphasis leads me inevitably on to controversial ground; if my evaluation of some aspects of the region's past or of the contemporary socio-economic situation seems at times debatable, I can only claim that it grows out of some eight years' discontinuous field work in the area, out of my observations in Southeast Asia and other parts of the Third World, and out of discussions with friends in many parts of the region. I would record my gratitude to these friends and at the same time absolve them from any responsibility for such errors of interpretation as may occur in the volume.

I would record my special gratitude to Professor Robert Ho of Kuala Lumpur; Professor Rudi Wikkramatileke and Mr. Sambendan Vedagiri of Singapore; His Excellency Chau Seng and M. Charles Meyer of Phnom Penh; M. Le Van Thuoi and M. Tran Nguyen of Hanoi; and His Excellency Phoumi Vongvichit of Vientiane. To these, to my interpreters and other friends I would express my warm appreciation.

I would also acknowledge with gratitude the help of Mrs. Joan Elmes who typed—and retyped—the various drafts of the volume; of Mrs. Barbara Winchester who has been responsible for the maps and cartograms; of Mrs. Jean Benfield who prepared the plates from my original Kodachromes; and of Miss Ann Stewart who compiled the Index. Their help has greatly lightened my work and I am deeply appreciative.

Finally, without the periods of leave granted me by the University the field work on which this book is based would have been impossible. It is appropriate that I should acknowledge the generous understanding of the necessity for field work which the Council of Victoria University of Wellington, and the Vice-Chancellor, Dr. J. Williams, have shown; this understanding has been a major factor in the development of geography at Victoria University.

KEITH BUCHANAN

CHAPTER 1

Perspective

THE SOUTHEAST Asian world, within the limits shown on map 25, has an area of some one and a half million square miles (almost equally divided between mainland Southeast Asia and insular Southeast Asia) and a population of over 220 millions. Its area is thus less than half that of the United States though if the landlocked seas and island-sprinkled straits which make up an important part of the region's living space are included the areal discrepancy is much reduced. And its total population is not only greater than that of the United States, its growth rate (or its potential population) is very much greater. United Nations population estimates suggest that by the end of the century it may well have a population of some 548 millions, as against an estimated population for the United States *and* Canada of 326 millions. In terms of area and population the region is important; it is likely to be of even greater importance in the years ahead for *by the end of this century it may well contain almost one-twelfth of the population of the globe.*

It is important also in terms of its resource endowment. The term 'The Tropical Far East' has been used by some writers as a regional label and this serves to draw attention to one aspect of its resource pattern—it is a major source of tropical raw materials, not only foodstuffs but also industrial crops such as rubber and fibres. Its development as a supplier of these commodities was greatly aided by its physical geography—for it is the only major tropical area which enjoys a high degree of accessibility. Development of tropical Africa or tropical America is hindered by their relative inaccessibility. The Amazon has never developed as a major transport route; the Congo and other central African rivers suffer from breaks in profile which make rail links a necessary, costly, and time-consuming supplement to water transport. This land-locked character of the two other great tropical regions stands in sharp contrast to conditions in the Asiatic tropics. Here the South China Sea and its extensions, the Java Sea, the Celebes Sea and the Banda Sea, fragment the southeastern margin of tropical Asia into a complex pattern of peninsulas and islands, of land-girdled seas and sea-connecting straits. The whole area enjoys a high degree of accessibility by water and this is increased by the navigable lower courses of its great rivers which probe deep into the heart of mainland Southeast Asia. Since, from the early seventeenth century, the military and commercial power of Europe was largely based on sea-power, this accessibility helps to explain the early integration of much of the area into the commercial, then colonial, empires of the Western European powers. The resources of the area—its spices and rare woods, its alluvial or volcanic soils suited to rice or to plantation crops, later its minerals and its labouring masses—could be readily integrated into the economies of the colonial powers. And at a period when military power meant sea-power, this same accessibility rendered the whole region vulnerable to the gunboat type of diplomacy and so to Western political pressure. . . .

The events of the Second World War drove home forcibly the economic and political significance of the region and events during the last two decades have increasingly underlined the geopolitical significance of Southeast Asia. The collapse of the old colonial system and the re-emergence of the former colonial dependencies as independent states would have inevitably brought new stresses. These stresses have, however, been greatly magnified by three sets of factors: first, by the apparent failure of Western-style free enterprise to solve the problem of under-development in areas such as Southeast Asia and by the increasing shift towards planned and socialist-type economies; this trend is evident throughout the whole of the Third World[1]

[1] French term applied to the bloc of emergent nations; by analogy with the Third Estate in pre-Revolutionary France 'the mass which was at one and the same time almost everything and almost nothing' (A. Sauvy). The First World is represented by the industrialised nations of Euro-America; the Second World by the communist countries of the U.S.S.R. and Eastern Europe. The Asian socialist countries are usually excluded from the 'Third World' even though the problems they had to face were very similar to those facing the other emergent nations.

and, though in many cases it is simply a response to economic realities, the West has tended to regard it with suspicion, as due to political subversion which must be countered. Secondly, the coming to power of communist governments in China (1949) and North Vietnam (1954); this introduced a new element into the Southeast Asian scene for these countries can now offer a model of economic development more successful than the traditional free enterprise model offered by the West, while their attitude to national liberation movements strengthens the hand of all those groups in Southeast Asia who are dissatisfied with existing political and economic structures. Thirdly, and closely linked with this development, the active extension of America's military perimeter to take in part at least of Southeast Asia. At the time of writing this perimeter runs from South Korea and Japan, through Okinawa and Taiwan, through the American-administered parts of South Vietnam to Thailand; it is backed by the Philippines and Australia–New Zealand and by the British forces based on Hong Kong and Singapore. Geopolitically, then, we may say three forces converge or clash in Southeast Asia: the struggle of the emergent countries to assert their individualities and achieve an economic breakthrough; the influence of the Asian communist régimes and, thirdly, the attempts of the West, and especially the United States, to channel the first force and counteract the second. The chaotic and strife-torn history of parts of Southeast Asia since 1949 results from this clash; it is a clash which exists in a latent or overt form in every part of the Third World but its impact in Southeast Asia is aggravated by the close geographical juxtaposition of the major protagonists.

MAJOR CHARACTERISTICS

We have already set Southeast Asia into its global context in one way by describing it as a tropical area; from this tropical character derive some of the basic problems of the region—the instability of many of its soils and the problem of maintaining soil fertility, the heavy incidence of certain human diseases, to take but two examples. These are important aspects and we shall be returning to them later. Yet perhaps even more important than its physical character, or even its human

Southeast Asia in its Third World Context

In these four cartograms the area of each country is shown proportional to its population; the four diagrams set the region into its global context.

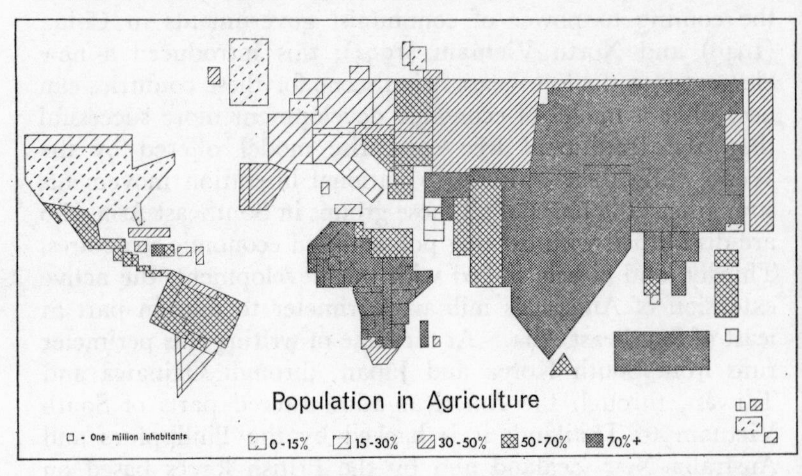

1 Population engaged in agriculture, illustrating the undiversified character of most Southeast Asian economies; the only notable—and partial exceptions—are Singapore–Malaya and the Philippines.

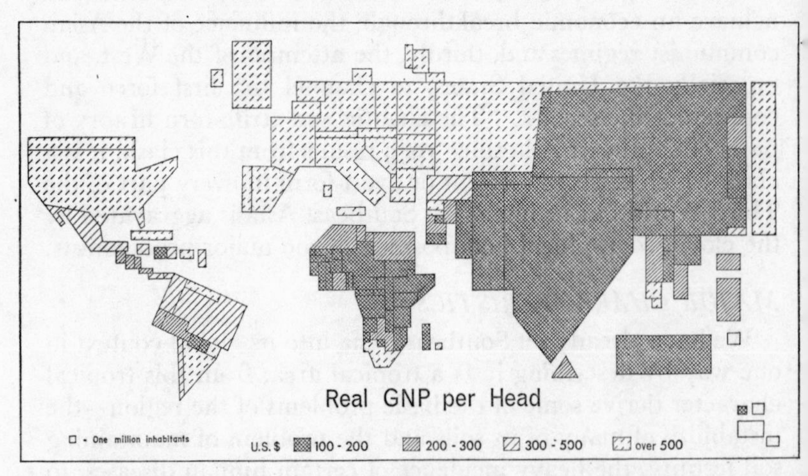

2 Real G.N.P. per Head. The problem of poverty which Southeast Asia shares with other Third World countries is illustrated by the figures for Gross National Product per head. For Indonesia and half the population of mainland Southeast Asia this is under $(US)100.

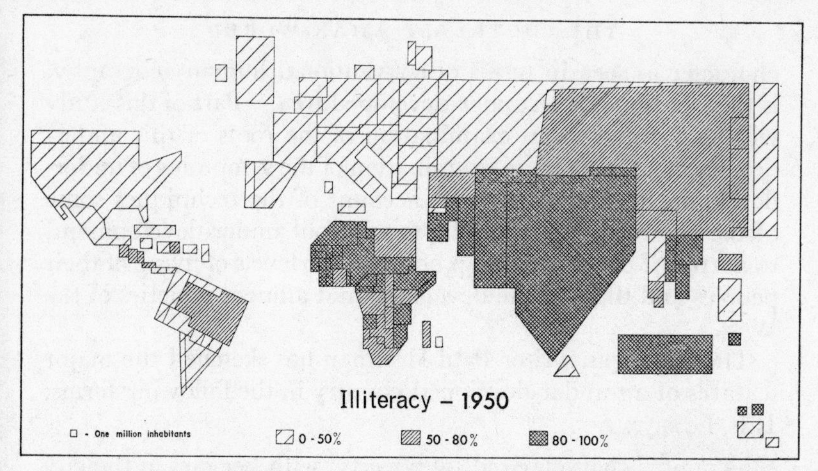

3 Illiteracy 1950. One of the major indices of under-development is illiteracy; this stands as a major barrier to modernisation and development. Over much of Southeast Asia four out of every five persons are illiterate.

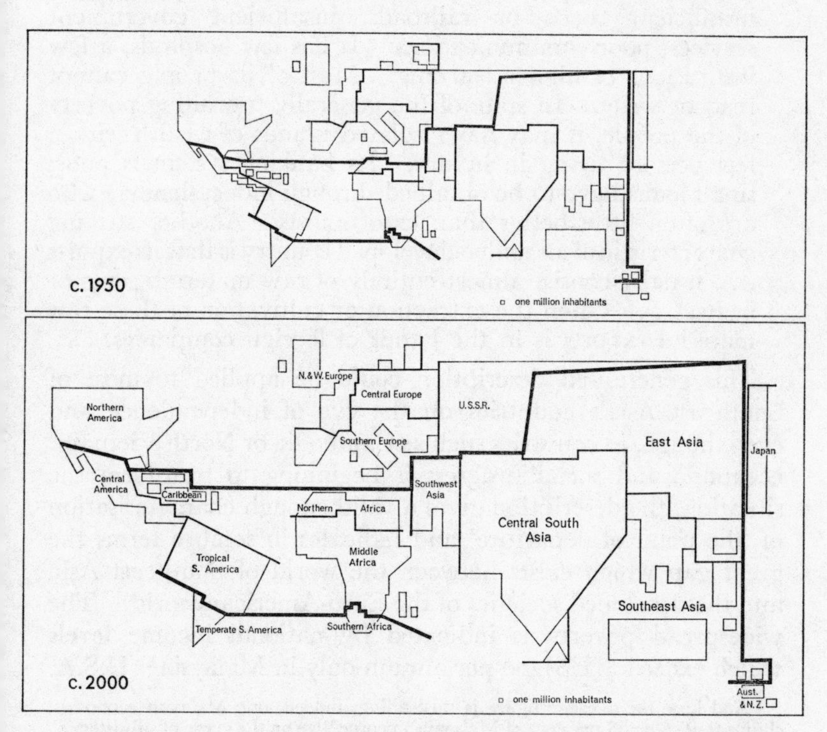

4 The Expansion of Population 1950–2000. Area of countries is in both these maps proportional to population. By the end of the century Southeast Asia is likely to have a population of half a billion people.

character as seen in terms of conventional human geography, is the fact that it is an under-developed area. Part of this study will be devoted to an examination of the roots of this under-development, part to an examination of the symptoms of under-development, and part to an account of the techniques some of the countries are adopting to wipe out under-development, to narrow if possible the gap between the levels of living of their peoples and those of the developed and affluent societies of the West.

The American writer Paul Hoffman has sketched the major features of an under-developed country in the following terms: It is, he says:

> a country characterized by poverty, with beggars in the city and villages eking out a bare subsistence in the rural areas. It is a country lacking in factories of its own, usually with inadequate supplies of power and light. It usually has insufficient roads or railroads, insufficient government services, poor communications. It has few hospitals, a few institutions of higher learning. Most of its people cannot read or write. In spite of the generally prevailing poverty of the people, it may have isolated islands of wealth with a few persons living in luxury. Its banking system is poor; small loans have to be obtained through money-lenders who are often little better than extortionists. Another striking characteristic of an under-developed country is that its exports . . . usually consist almost entirely of raw materials, ores or fruits. . . . Often the extraction or cultivation of these raw material exports is in the hands of foreign companies. . . .

This generalised description could be applied to most of Southeast Asia's countries on the eve of independence and even though, in countries such as Cambodia or North Vietnam, economic and social progress is beginning to transform the situation, the description gives a valid enough characterisation of 'the point of departure' and indicates in sombre terms the great gap which exists between the world of Southeast Asia and the developed societies of the Euro-American world. The widespread poverty is indicated by national income levels which exceed $(US)200 per annum only in Malaysia[1] (U.S.A.

[1] And here the average figure is misleading; indeed, one Malayan economist claims that some 98 per cent of Malaysia's people 'live on the verge of subsistence'.

$(US)2,108). Economic diversification is, with the exception of Malaysia, North Vietnam and the Philippines, still in its infancy. The agricultural sector of the economy is grossly inflated and polarised between inefficient production of food for local consumption and specialised production of export crops for the world market; moreover, given the relative stagnation in levels of food production, the proportion of imports represented by foodstuffs is as high in Malaya or Indonesia as in the industrialised nations of northwest Europe. The dangerously specialised—and hence vulnerable—character of these economies (or 'semi-economies', see p. 79) is underlined by the dependence of their export trade on a very limited range of commodities: three major primary products make up 90 per cent of the exports of Malaya and over 75 per cent of the exports of Cambodia, Thailand and South Vietnam. Modern industry is poorly developed; it employs less than 1·5 million people and, indeed, the tertiary sector (service and commerce) employs two-and-a-half times as many people as secondary industry. And, as a consequence and a cause of poverty, social services are only now beginning to take shape: in 1950 only Thailand could show a literacy rate of over 50 per cent and as late as 1960 Laos had only two doctors and Indonesia a ratio of one doctor to 70,000 people (cp. U.S.A. 1:800)....

Figure 3 presents in graphic form some of the economic and social indices which differentiate Southeast Asia most clearly from a developed nation such as the United Kingdom; that this under-development has a human cost is emphasised by the data for infantile mortality presented in this diagram: even on a conservative basis the loss of young lives in the first year of life is almost four times as heavy in Southeast Asia as in the United Kingdom.

The major features of the human geography of Southeast Asia, and the major problems faced by the new states of Southeast Asia, arise from this fact of under-development; by comparison with the developed nations of the West their social and economic structures have been warped and retarded and these processes have resulted in an impoverished and marginal quality of life for the great majority of their peoples.

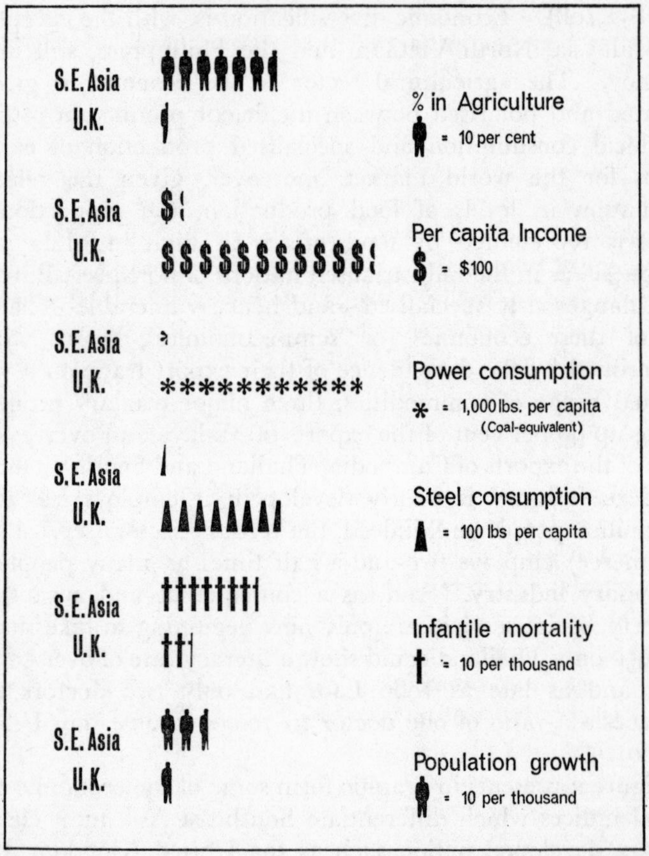

S.E. Asia
U.K.
% in Agriculture
= 10 per cent

S.E. Asia
U.K.
Per capita Income
$ = $100

S.E. Asia
U.K.
Power consumption
* = 1,000 lbs. per capita
(Coal-equivalent)

S.E. Asia
U.K.
Steel consumption
= 100 lbs per capita

S.E. Asia
U.K.
Infantile mortality
= 10 per thousand

S.E. Asia
U.K.
Population growth
= 10 per thousand

5 Contrasts in Living Levels between Southeast Asia and the United Kingdom. In this cartogram selected indices illustrate the great gap in material and social conditions between an 'affluent' nation such as the U.K. and the emerging countries of Southeast Asia.

Superficial observers have been inclined to explain away this backwardness as the result of a tropical environment or the alleged lethargy of the tropical peoples. That such environmentalist-racist explanations have little validity is clearly indicated by the history of the region which demonstrates the earlier existence in the region of developed and sophisticated societies; it also suggests, as we shall see later (pp. 77–82) that one of the major causes of the region's backwardness was the warping and retardation of economic and social development resulting from the impact of European colonial rule.

SOUTHEAST ASIA: 'Pre-developed' rather than 'Under-developed'

The term 'under-developed' has been used above to characterise the Southeast Asian social and economic scene and this follows closely the customary usage. Yet there is a great deal of truth in the contention of the French geographer Jean Chesneaux that many of what we term 'under-developed' societies are in reality nothing of the sort; rather are they 'pre-developed' societies which had attained a high degree of cultural, economic and political development long before these things were attained by Western Europe. Their relative backwardness today, measured in material terms such as standard of living or degree of economic diversification, is due in part at least to the fact that their later development was cut short by the colonial system imposed on them by Europe in the eighteenth and nineteenth centuries. The economic gap which today separates the affluent nations of Western Europe from the nations of Southeast Asia is thus of relatively recent origin; it certainly cannot be explained away simply in terms of the difficulties of enervating quality of the tropical environment or some sort of intellectual inferiority on the part of the tropical peoples. . . .

It may seem unnecessary to insist on this yet it is central to the whole question of economic development. For if it could be shown that the 'backwardness' of Southeast Asia (or of the tropical world generally) is indeed the result of the relentless pressure of a marginal environment or of 'racial' factors, then the whole process of economic development would be immensely protracted and costly; given the rapid rate of population growth in Southeast Asia it might well prove an impossible task. But if the poverty is due largely to historical factors, then man who created the conditions which led *to* poverty can equally certainly initiate the development which will lead *out* of poverty.

The historical record provides ample evidence that Chesneaux's term 'pre-developed' is a more accurate designation for Southeast Asia than the more usual 'under-developed'. The

Hinduised trading empires of Sri Vijaya (seventh to thirteenth Centuries) and Majapahit (thirteenth and fourteenth Centuries) were contemporaneous with the chaos of the European Dark Ages and the beginnings of feudalism; at a time when Western Europe was a patchwork of small and struggling feudal principalities they had welded much of Southeast Asia into a loosely structured but culturally and commercially sophisticated unity. In Cambodia, the construction of the great religious monument known as the Bayon (part of the Angkor complex; see Plate 1) was begun perhaps a century after the Bayeux tapestry was woven in Western Europe; its bas-reliefs (Plate 2) give a picture of a rich and flourishing rural life and comparison with the scenes depicted on the celebrated Norman tapestry suggest that life in Cambodia at that date was a good deal more settled and civilised than in the state William the Conqueror had established in England. The stonework on later monuments on the Angkor site captures the spirit of a polished and luxury-loving society and this society was described at the end of the thirteenth century by Marco Polo and the Chinese traveller Chou Ta-kuan. The Khmer civilisation they describe was, at its upper levels, a good deal more cultured and refined and, at its lower levels, more solicitous of the welfare of the common man than was the civilisation of contemporary medieval Europe we can glimpse in the literature of Chaucer or Villon a century later, or in the films of Ingmar Bergman. . . . And such data as we have suggests that as late as the eighteenth century the common man in Southeast Asia had a level of living not greatly different from that of his fellow man in Western Europe; for the upper classes life may well have been more refined and comfortable in Southeast Asia than in Western Europe.

'It is,' says Pierre Moussa, 'only comparatively recently that the West has been so far ahead of other nations in regard to economic development . . . the differential between the West and the rest of the world, seen on the scale of human history, is quite a recent event. In a few decades it has reached extraordinary proportions.'

That Southeast Asia is today what we term an 'underdeveloped' region is due to two things: first, the sudden technological progress of Europe following the Industrial Revolution and related changes which enabled her to draw ahead of the rest of humanity; secondly, and closely related, the destructive impact of a militarily superior Europe whose colonial policy, as we shall see later (pp. 74–82) destroyed the old balance of

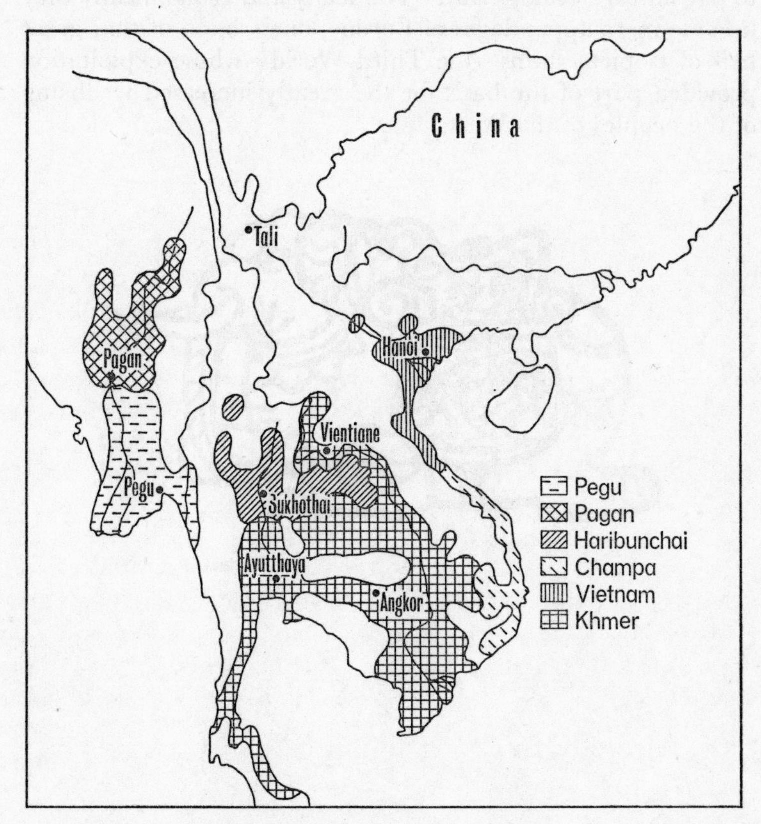

6 Major States of Southeast Asia, *c.* 1300. The maps show the situation at the height of Khmer power and before the Hinduised state of Champa was absorbed by the southward-advancing Annamese.

life in these lands. These areas, like the rest of the tropics, became simply raw material-producing areas—and markets—for the developing economies of the West. Their own economy disintegrated and the gap in level of living between the peoples of Southeast Asia and the peoples of Europe began to widen and has continued to widen ever since. The Southeast Asian countries became, in absolute and relative terms, 'under-developed'; indeed, it is no exaggeration to claim, as some have claimed, that *their* under-development was the price they had to pay for *our* development. Politically and economically they became mere appendages of Europe, one section of that great belt of tropical slums—the Third World—whose exploitation provided part of the basis for the greatly increased wellbeing of the peoples of the West.

CHAPTER 2

Diversity in Unity

DISCUSSING THE human ecology of Southeast Asia,[1] E. H. G. Dobby, has drawn attention to the constant convergence of peoples on this frayed-out southeastern margin of Eurasia. In explaining these movements he draws attention to three sets of factors:

(i) the high degree of accessibility of the area, especially by water.
(ii) the location of the region between the two great 'culture-worlds' of India and China. Intervening barriers of mountain or jungle (Figures 15 & 18) directed contacts either northwestwards from China towards the Middle East along the line of the Silk Road or, alternatively, southwards along the seaways of the Malayan world; with improved navigation techniques this southern sea-route became increasingly important.
(iii) the fact that the relatively empty lands of Southeast Asia represented for the rice-growing peoples of East Asia a pioneer fringe area; this acted as a magnet to migrants, attracting settlers in much the same way that the American prairies attracted settlers from the closely-settled Atlantic sea-board.

To these three sets of factors we may add a fourth—the expansion of the Chinese (Han) people, pushing southwards as population grew from their cradle area in the valley of the Yellow River, filling up subtropical and tropical south China and providing, by this pressure, the momentum which set off great ripples of migration which affected the whole of the

[1] In *Geographical Journal 108* (1946), pp. 40–57.

tropical Far East. Over many hundreds of years the pre-Chinese peoples of central and south China were displaced into the upland areas or in the direction of the Indochinese lands far to the south and their pressure in turn triggered off tribal movements which affected the whole of mainland Southeast Asia and the adjoining island world.

The general result of these movements is reflected in the great diversity, racial and cultural, of Southeast Asia's population (Plates 3–10). Mixing of peoples of the most diverse physical types has been taking place over many millennia; so, too, has the inter-weaving of many diverse cultural elements.

In racial terms, the earliest inhabitants of the Southeast Asian world appear to have been negritos, small-statured, woolly-haired, dark-skinned peoples represented today by the Semang and the Aeta; these are primitive food-collectors dwelling in the forest fastnesses of Malaya and the Philippines. Their numbers are infinitesimal—possibly 2,000 in Malaya—but, as a result of past race-mixing, they have contributed to racial make-up of many Southeast Asian peoples. Veddid elements, related to the peoples of parts of southern India and, more distantly, to the Australian aborigine, have been present in the area from very early times. They are today represented by groups such as the Senoi of Malaya, wavy-haired, narrow-headed, dark-skinned agriculturalists practising shifting cultivation. And, as in the case of the negrito type, this type has mixed extensively with other groups and is to be found, in varying degrees of dilution, over much of Southeast Asia. The basal population in much of the area appears to belong to the Nesiot or Brown Race; these are olive- or dark-skinned peoples, with wavy hair and narrow nose and represent the easternmost extension of the Mediterranean race whose extension is from Western Europe, through the Mediterranean and Middle East to northern India. The group appears to have diffused into Southeast Asia from the northwest and may have been the bearer of the megalithic culture of Assam and Chota Nagpur. Today its extent is from southern China (many of the minority peoples are non-Mongoloid and belong to this group) to the Indonesian islands. The last group to enter the area consists of the broad-headed, straight-haired Alpine-Mongoloid peoples who moved southwards in a series of migrations from the second millennium B.C., displacing or

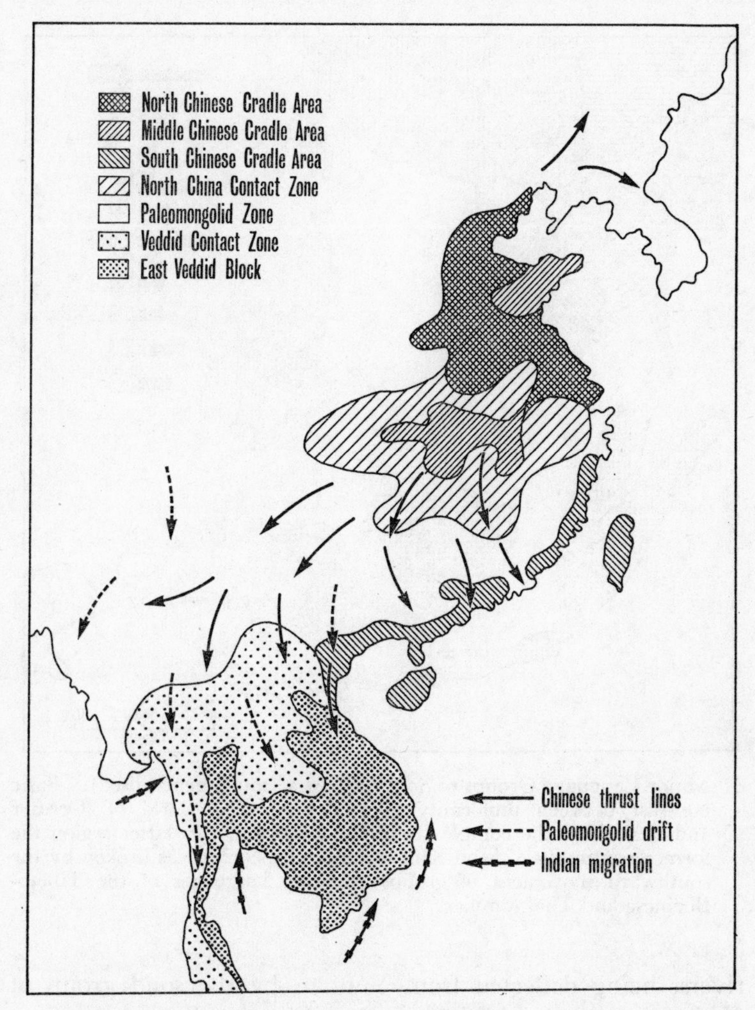

7 Dynamics of Early Population Movement in East Asia (second to third millennium B.C.). Illustrating the overspilling and southward thrust of migration from the three Chinese cradle areas and the consequent pressures on the darker Veddid peoples who occupied most of mainland Southeast Asia (after von Eickstedt).

mixing with the wavy- or kinky-haired aborigines. These peoples appear to have spread down the upper valleys of the Irrawaddy, which they reached *c.* 600 B.C., and other

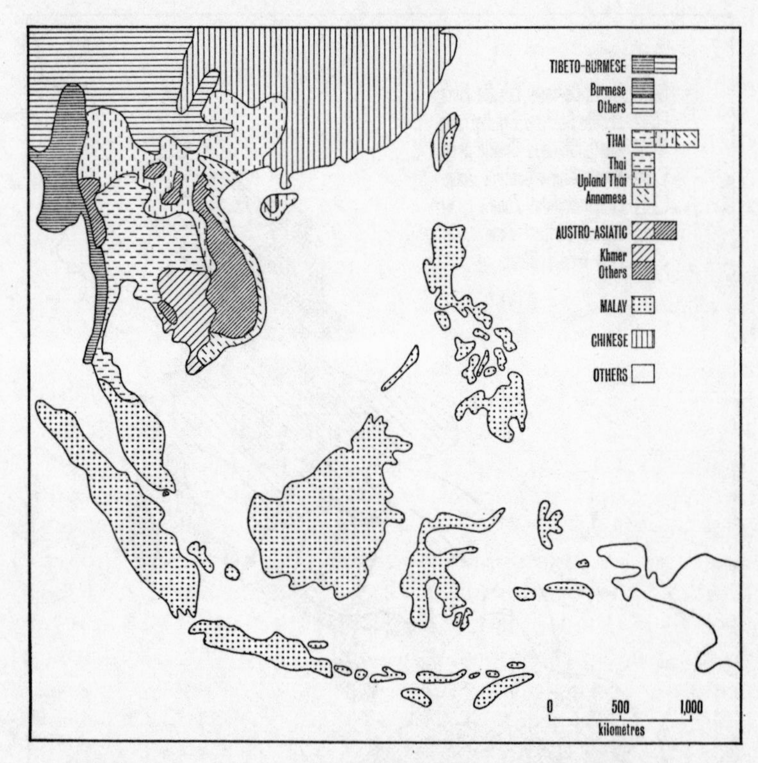

8 Major Language Groups of Southeast Asia (much generalised). Basic contrast between uniformity of Malay-speaking world of 'Greater Indonesia' and the complexity of the mainland. In latter region the former continuity of Mon-Khmer speaking peoples was broken by the southward movement of groups speaking languages of the Tibeto-Burmese and Thai families.

rivers, being deflected from Yunnan by the solid group of Nesiot peoples established there. In spreading south they have been modified by long centuries of race-mixing with earlier groups and this modification increases southwards; only in the north are relatively pure Mongoloid forms to be found. Mongoloid or partially-Mongoloid elements are especially important in the coastal areas, the older groups having been pushed towards the forested and upland regions of the interior. This southward drift of Mongoloid peoples has continued up to the present time and the migration of Chinese into the area in the last century, in response to the demands for plantation and mine labour and the new commercial opportunities, can be regarded as merely the continuation of this thousand-year old overflow towards the tropics.

EARLY CULTURAL INFLUENCES

Upon this racial diversity is superimposed a great diversity of linguistic groups; these are of major importance because, in Southeast Asia as in Europe, language has been an important focusing point in the emergence of new nationalisms. At the beginning of recorded history the mainland appears to have been occupied by peoples speaking languages of the Mon-Khmer family; at this date languages of this family were dominant not only in Southeast Asia but over the whole of southern China as far north as the valley of the Yangtse-kiang. This dominance of the so-called Austro-Asiatic group of languages on the mainland was paralleled by the dominance in the Malay peninsula and the island world beyond of Malayo-Polynesian languages belonging to the Austronesian group; these overlapped only slightly into the Indochinese peninsula where the Chams spoke a Malayo-Polynesian language. The linguistic homogeneity of mainland Southeast Asia has been shattered, during the last 2,000 years, by the introduction into the area of Sino-Tibetan languages, carried by immigrant peoples—Burmese, Thai and Vietnamese—moving outward from the cradle areas of the Irrawaddy valley, the plain of the Menam and the Red River lowland respectively. The earlier Austro-Asiatic-speaking peoples were pushed into the forested uplands (e.g. the Annamite Cordillera) and with the sole exception of Cambodia the major lowlands of Southeast Asia are today dominated by peoples speaking languages of the Sino-Tibetan group. In the island world of Southeast Asia and in the peninsula of Malaya the Austronesian languages held their ground though there has been considerable evolution and regional differentiation within the general family so that Indonesian Malay today consists of some 25 languages and 250 dialects. The vocabulary of the various languages was enriched, and the form of many stabilised, by external impacts, notably the impact of India.

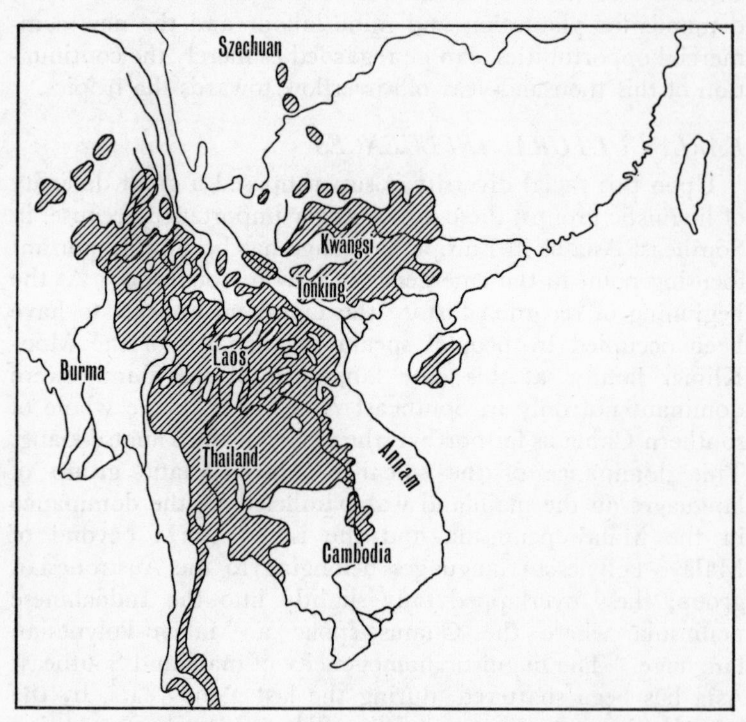

9 Distribution of Peoples Speaking Languages of the Thai Group. Note the way in which this pattern cuts across the political frontiers of the colonial and post-colonial period.

Indian scripts were introduced and now form the basis of Cambodian, Burman, Shan, Thai and Laotian scripts: they were used also in some of the regional languages of Indonesia though in Atjeh, in the coastal areas, and in peninsular Malaya these were superseded by Arabic script. Vietnamese formerly used a script based on Chinese ideographs but this has been superseded by a Roman script and this script is today the standard script for the national languages of Indonesia, Malaya and the Philippines.

The contrast between mainland Southeast Asia and the islands appears also in the field of religion, the mainland

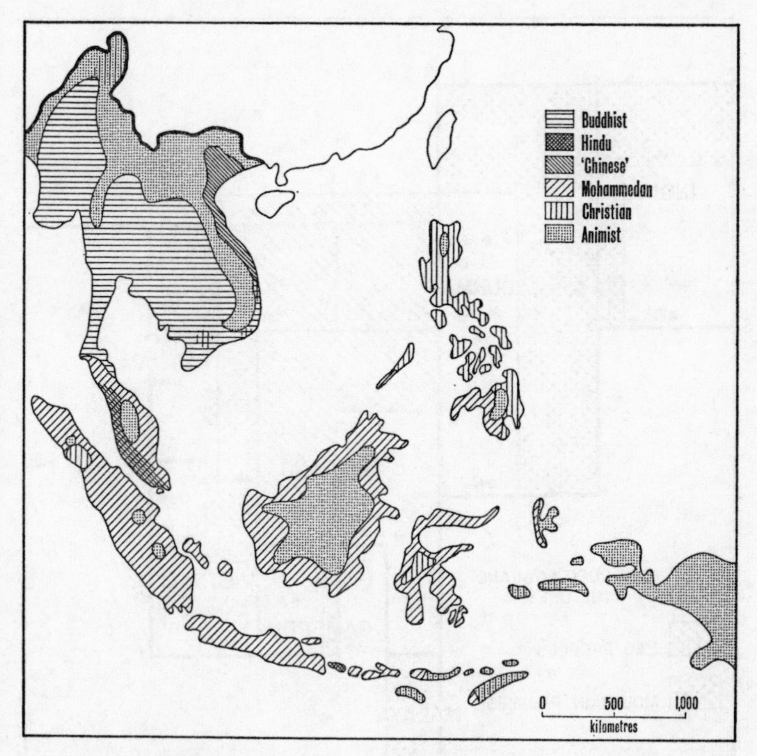

10 The Religions of Southeast Asia. Emphasising the basic contrast between the Malaysian world, dominated by Islam, and Mainland Southeast Asia which is largely Buddhist in its religious affiliation. Note the survival of Hinduism in the island of Bali and the important Christian communities of the Philippines and, to a lesser extent, parts of upland Southeast Asia and Indonesia.

peoples being largely Buddhist in faith while those of the islands have been Islamised. Throughout the whole of the area, however, there is a tendency to syncretism; later religions blended with earlier faiths as, for example, in the cult of Siva-Buddha in Java or the more recent and complex syncrtisms of South Vietnam (e.g. the Cao-Daist sect). Moreover, in the processes of transplantation and maturing in Southeast Asia religions have tended to lose much of their fierce and narrow dogmatism, to become softened if not attenuated.

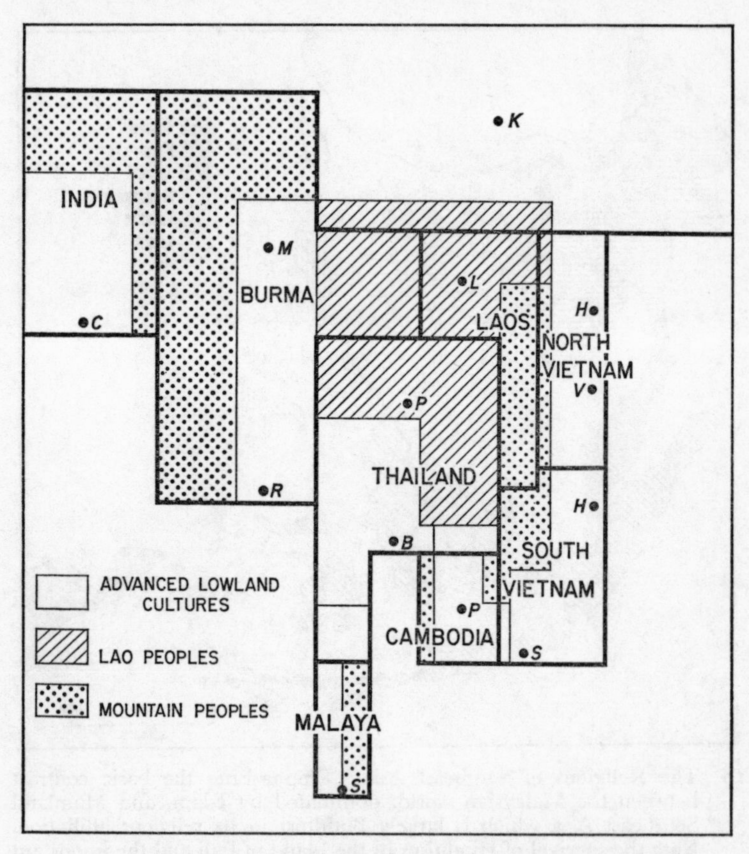

11 Cartogram illustrating Complex Ethnic Composition of the Countries of Southeast Asia. Each country consists of a core area, inhabited by the dominant group possessing an advanced culture, and a periphery inhabited by more backward tribal groups.

As early racial groups survive in a relatively pure form in the remote and forested interiors so, too, do the earlier animistic beliefs; moreover, just as these early human groups blended with newcomers in the more accessible lowlands and coast plains, so have these earlier animistic beliefs survived as a substratum on which later and more developed faiths were superimposed.

By the second century of our era, small colonies of Indian merchants were established around the shores of the Southeast Asian Mediterranean and this commercial contact was followed by the introduction of Indian religions—Hinduism and Buddhism. The process of effective 'Indianisation' in the field of religion may have been largely concentrated around these trading ports and in the interior the new religions may have been much diluted by blending with earlier animistic faiths. What does seem clear is that for a long period Hinduism and Buddhism co-existed happily in Southeast Asia and that one of the physical expressions of this dual presence are the great cities of this earlier period—Angkor, and some of the Indonesian and Burmese cities—which were 'built as models of Hindu-Buddhist cosmology' (C. A. Fisher). Today Hinduism survives as a living religion only on the island of Bali, though the former extent and influence of this religion is indicated by the great temple-complexes whose distribution extends from the mainland down into the island world of Indonesia. Buddhism reached the Empires of Fu-nan and Champa in the second century A.D., spreading to Malaya and the adjoining shores of the Indonesian islands three centuries later.[1] In succeeding centuries it lost its hold on the Malay world though it has remained to this day the dominant religion of most of mainland Southeast Asia; in the last decade or so it has emerged as a significant political force; both Burma and Cambodia have evolved indigenous 'Buddhist socialisms', based largely on the social and economic teachings of Buddhism and in South Vietnam the Buddhists have played an important role in the political affairs of the country since 1960.

The major exception to the dominance of Buddhism in the non-Malay world is to be found in the Annamese lands where nearly a thousand years of Chinese control resulted in the 'Sinicisation' of Annamese culture; in the religious field this expressed itself in the increasing domination of what may, for

[1] For maps illustrating the spread of Buddhism see E. Zürcher, *Buddhism* (New York, 1962).

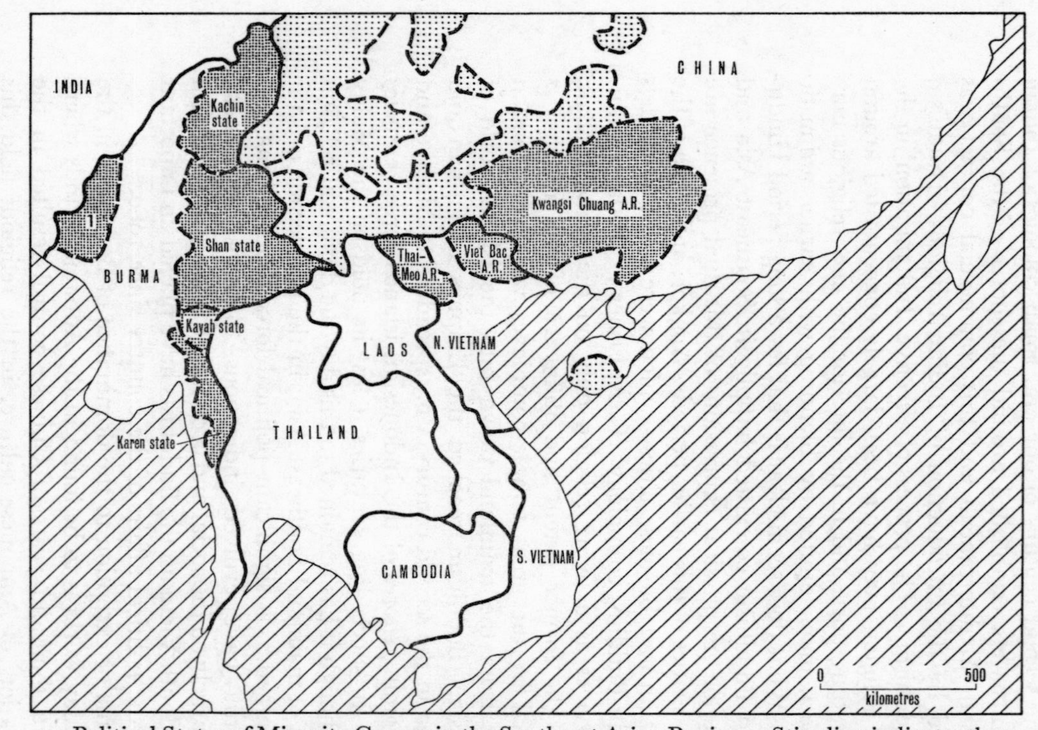

12 Political Status of Minority Groups in the Southeast Asian Region. Stippling indicates those regions within which minority peoples possess some degree of autonomy; dark stipple: Autonomous Regions within the Chinese People's Republic and the Democratic Republic of North Vietnam and non-Burmese States of the Union of Burma (1 = Special District of the Chins); light stipple: Autonomous Chou or Autonomous Area within the Chinese People's Republic.

want of a better description, be called the 'Chinese religion'. This is an amalgam of animist, Taoist and Confucian ideas and it may be that, as Richard Harris has argued, this legacy of Confucianism ('a temporal doctrine of the state and society') provides conditions more favourable to the acceptance of authoritarian patterns of government than the politically 'more open' societies of Indianised Southeast Asia. It is, he points out, 'only within east Asian civilisation that communist governments have been established';[1] he goes on to argue that the creation of an 'Indochina' by the French blurred the fundamental division between the Sinicised world and the Indianised world of Southeast Asia and that many of the West's problems in the area stem from an inability to recognise the political significance of this divide.

The impact of Islam introduced a new and important element of diversity into the region. The spread of the new religion may have been an indirect consequence of trade for, during the Middle Ages, there were important trading contacts between Southeast Asia, India and the Middle East and 'Arab' traders, using Chinese junks, were acting as intermediaries in the trade between Europe and the Far East. Such groups installed themselves at many points along the sea-ways of Southern Asia; they included many Gujeratis from northwest India so that the Islam they introduced was very much an Indianised Islam. Islamised states began to appear in Sumatra in the middle of the thirteenth century; expansion continued during the next 200 years and in 1450 reached Malacca which became a major port and centre for Gujerati missionary activity. As in the earlier case of Hinduism, intermarriage played an important role in the extension of the new faith and the marriage of Moslems into the princely families of the region was a significant factor in establishing Islam among the upper classes. Its geographical diffusion was uneven; except in Malaya it did not succeed in displacing Buddhism on the mainland; in the Philippines its advance was checked by the Spaniards who established in the northern part of the island group an outpost of Spanish Catholicism.

Nevertheless, Islam brought about the final collapse of the

[1] Richard Harris *Independence and After* (London, 1962), p. 7.

empire of Majapahit in 1520 and by the end of the century most of the islands were converted to the new faith. Only in Bali did Hinduism survive, as it survives to this day. With local exceptions, Southeast Asian Islam is a 'diluted' Islam, compromising with, co-existing with, elements of the earlier animistic or Hindu beliefs. Except in Malaya, Achin, Minangkabau, and Mindanao the Arabic script has not displaced the earlier Indian scripts; in social matters, such as inheritance customs, Islamic and pre-Islamic codes still come into conflict as in Malaya. But the long period of Islamisation has left a major legacy in Southeast Asia in the shape of a solid bloc of close on 100 million Moslems, one-half of the population of Southeast Asia and almost one-fifth of the world's Moslem population.

LATER INFLUENCES

The major later influences have been those of China and of Europe.

The Chinese influence has been massive and protracted and has manifested itself especially in the fields of material culture and economics. To quote Charles Robequain, the Chinese 'taught the natives how to manufacture and use fire-arms. Their influence appears not only in dress, boats and shapes of sails but also in certain patterns in the plastic arts. . . . The native dialects are enriched with many words borrowed from Chinese. . . .' The areal extent of this influence is evident from the distribution of, for example, the Chinese-type plough; it is widespread in Vietnam, the Philippines and North Borneo but is replaced by the Indian-type plough in Java and Sumatra, Cambodia and Laos. Even more important has been the large-scale migration of Chinese which, in the late nineteenth and early twentieth century, was set in motion by the European development of the mining and plantation industries in Southeast Asia. Many came as indentured labourers, to work in the tin mines and the rubber plantations; most came from the crowded coastlands of southeastern China and the scale of this migratory flow prompted Pierre Gourou to observe that 'Southeast Asia was a Chinese rather than a European colonial domain'. The Chinese community in the Nan-yang (lit. the

Southern Sea) today numbers at least ten millions though intermarriage with the local inhabitants (as in Thailand) makes any meaningful enumeration precarious. It is almost impossible to generalise about the character of the migration or the role of the group. Many came as labourers to areas being newly developed for export production (as western Malaya) others came as merchants to areas already closely settled (as Java); yet others came to areas little developed and thinly settled (as western Borneo). If any generalisation is permitted it is that they have constituted a 'middle group', between the peasant masses and the Western groups in control (or, in Thailand, the indigenous ruling group); that their commercial and economic drive has played a critical role in the development of the region; and that their very success, and the power which resulted from this success, have made them extremely vulnerable targets for the new (and often xenophobic) nationalisms of Southeast Asia (Plate 10).

The European impact has taken several forms. Actual settlement was, in pre-war days, on a small scale; it was probably of the order of 300,000 (many of whom were mixed bloods) as against some thirty times as many Chinese. Specific manifestations of this European impact will be examined later; here we may merely note its major manifestations. In the political field it resulted in a pattern of territorial units which had little relationship to the ethnic or historical conditions of the area; an excellent example is the arbitrary grouping of differing geographic regions, and of Hinduised, Sinicised and tribal peoples, which was former French Indochina. Economically, it meant that the development of the countries of Southeast Asia became subordinated to the needs of the metropolitan power; the development was not necessarily related in any way to local needs or aspirations and the resultant highly specialised economy (e.g. Malaya) was highly vulnerable to world trade fluctuations. This economic development was, moreover, largely unplanned and, concerned with maximising profits, extremely patchy in character so that the economic differentials between various regions was greatly increased. In the demographic field, the introduction of the beginnings of disease control, the encouragement of large-scale immigration to meet the needs of plantations and mines, and the incentive to have large families provided by the Dutch system of compulsory cultivation of certain crops—all these led to rapid population growth in certain areas; Malaya's population increased sixfold in fifty years and that of Java sevenfold in a century. Finally, European education, and the European political concepts (including more recently the concepts of Marxism) which this education made increasingly accessible, served ultimately to call into question and undermine the whole colonial order itself. From this to a reassertion of some of the values of traditional society, and the synthesis of these with concepts derived from the West, the step is small and today many Southeast Asian societies are at the stage of experimenting with new political forms based on such a reassertion and synthesis.

The cultural impact of the West today seems almost aggressively evident in many of Southeast Asia's cities, in their Western-style housing, the preoccupation of the wealthier members of the middle class with the status symbols of modern Western society, in films and in other mass media (Plates 38, 40, 44). Yet this 'Coca-colonisation' as one critic has termed it is limited in extent and has scarcely touched much of rural Southeast Asia. It is, moreover, a relatively recent phenomenon and as one Dutch scholar has said 'Until the turn of the twentieth century . . . it is difficult to find a positive Western cultural impact in Southeast Asia. Certainly, what there was did not compare in magnitude or indigenous sponsorship with the impact of Indian and Moslem culture.' Perhaps the one exception to this is the case of the Philippines. Here Catholic missionaries established solid control at an early date, limiting contact with Europe and America to one galleon a year between 1571 and 1811. To quote the same scholar: 'Carried by religious and educational channels, Spanish civilisation took a hold comparable to Indian and Moslem civilisation elsewhere in Southern Asia. The Filipinos adopted not only Catholicism, but European dress, music, dance and script . . . these influences persisted when the political bonds with the metropolitan country were broken.' Partly because of its longer historical span, the impact of missionary activity in the Philippines was much greater than in the Vietnamese lands; it brought not merely a new religion but a new society, adding thus a further element of complexity to an already complex human pattern in Southeast Asia.

CHAPTER 3

The Southeast Asian Setting

STRUCTURE AND climate give the Southeast Asian world a certain measure of unity; this was especially so in earlier times when sea-level was lower, the whole of the Sunda Platform was dry land, and Sumatra and Java were joined to the mainland. Under these conditions Java Man (*c.* 750,000 years ago) may well have wandered dry-foot from Malaya into what are now the Indonesian islands. Only with the melting of the ice-sheets and the consequent rise in sea-level were the Indies cut off from mainland Southeast Asia.

Two main elements enter into the structure of the area (Figure 13)—an old rigid block and, looped around its margins, a series of much younger fold-mountains. The former is variously termed 'Indo-Sinia' or the 'Indo-Malayan massif' and consists of ancient rocks folded along N–S lines in pre-Tertiary times. Subsequent erosion reduced much of the block to an area of subdued relief so that today it is typically occupied by either shallow seas, vast alluvial plains covering peneplained surfaces of igneous or metamorphic rocks, or moderately elevated hills or plateaux with mature topography. Locally, however, as in northern Burma, the uplift of the area during the Tertiary mountain-building period has resulted in a markedly more rugged relief. Economically, these older rocks are important for their mineral wealth; they are, for example, pierced by tin-bearing igneous intrusions while the younger rocks which occur in basins on the surface of the shield are important for oil and coal.

The second element is the Tertiary folded belt which consists of younger sedimentary rocks, chiefly sandstones and limestones, folded during the Alpine mountain-building period.

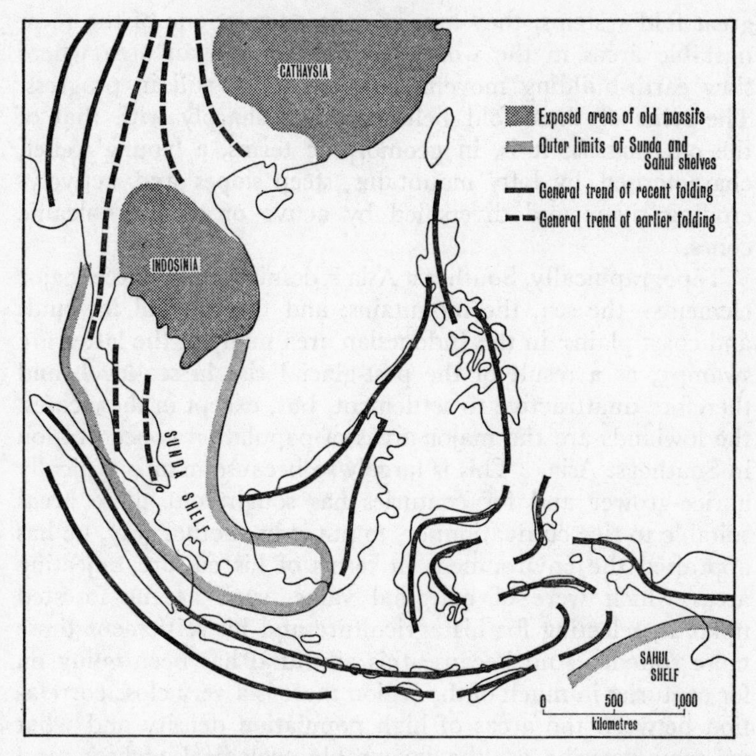

13 Major Structural Elements. Two major resistant massifs—those of Cathaysia and Indosinia—flanked by fold mountain belts of Tertiary or earlier age; these festoons of fold mountains are most complex in the eastern sector of Indonesia where the Alpine-Himalaya fold belt links up with the circum-Pacific fold belt.

This belt is flanked in the Indies and the Philippines by an important belt of active volcanoes; it also contains the region's major oil resources. Two main sections of this fold belt can be distinguished:

(*a*) The Alpine-Himalayan section which extends down through the Arakan Yoma, Sumatra and Java towards the Banda Arc;
(*b*) The circum-Pacific section which extends from North Borneo through the Philippines and Formosa to Japan.

The Indonesian islands lie close to the junction of these two great fold systems; they are, in consequence, one of the most unstable areas in the world tectonically and an area where slow earth-building movements seem to be still in progress. The relief of these fold belts contrasts sharply with that of the old massifs; it is, in geomorphic terms, a 'young' relief, characterised by lofty mountains, steep slopes and actively-eroding rivers and diversified by active or extinct volcanic cones.

Topographically, Southeast Asia is dominated by three major elements—the sea, the mountains, and the alluvial lowlands and coast plains; in the Indonesian area many of the latter are swampy, as a result of the post-glacial rise in sea-level, and therefore unattractive to settlement, but, except in these cases, the lowlands are the major areas of population concentration in Southeast Asia. This is largely so because man is typically a rice-grower and for centuries has sought out those areas suitable to rice cultivation; or, to put it in another way, he has appraised the environment in terms of his culture, rejecting areas which were of marginal value, such as the forested uplands, selecting for his agriculture and his settlement those more suited. And because this appraisal has been going on for centuries in much of the region there is a very close correlation between the areas of high population density and what we may describe as 'the favourable ecological niches'—and these are the lowlands, and especially those floored by recent alluvium.

The westernmost is the lowland of Burma. The northern and central sectors of this lowland are floored by Tertiary sediments which give rise to soils of only medium to low fertility; low rainfall further reduces the productivity of the area. Nevertheless, this area, possibly because of the ease with which its open forest cover could be cleared, was the heart of the Burmese kingdom. It was not until the British period that the richer 'aquatic fringe' of the lower delta was brought into cultivation, to become the major rice-producing region and the most densely-populated part of the country. Further east, the plain of Central Siam forms an almost dead-flat alluvial lowland. The lowland is wider than that of Central Burma; even at the northern end of the delta the inundated zone varies in width from 20 to 60 miles and fertility is maintained by the annual flooding. Nevertheless, this flooding is undependable from year to year and the annual rainfall (*c.* 40 inches) is below the optimum for successful rice-cultivation.

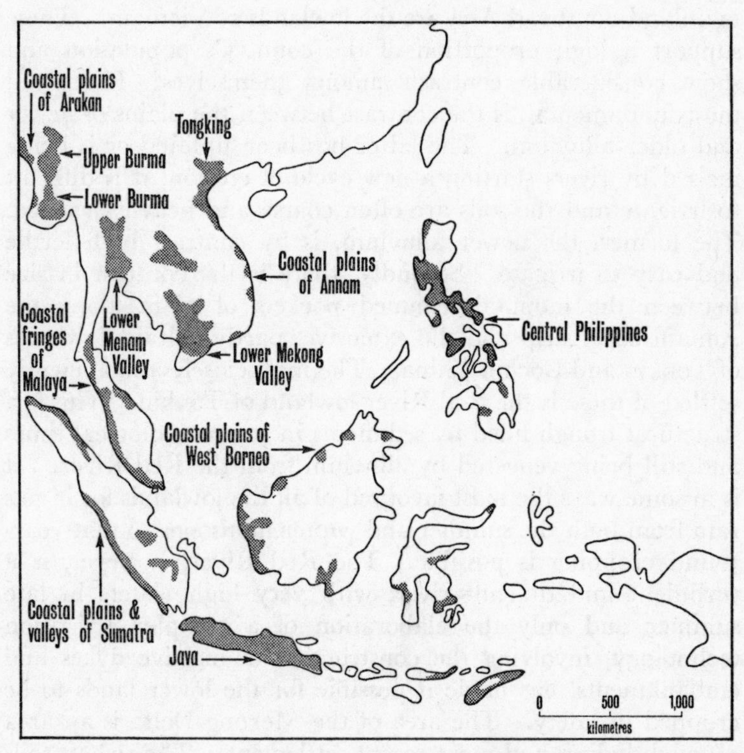

14 Favourable Ecological Niches. Illustrating in generalised form the major areas where environmental conditions (soils, rainfall or the possibilities of river-fed irrigation) seem most favourable to intensive agriculture.

Improved systems of water control would undoubtedly greatly increase the agricultural potential of the area but even without these it is one of the great rice-producing areas of the world and an area of high population density. In Cambodia the major rice-growing areas extend in the shape of an irregular and fragmented 'Y' along the valley of the Mekong and its western tributary, the Tonle Sap. These alluvial lowlands are flooded each year (Plate 15); the major zone of intensive cultivation and close settlement coincides with the area watered by these annual inundations, especially the area south of the capital of Phnom Penh. Finally, on the eastern margins of mainland Southeast Asia are the lowlands of Vietnam. These support a high proportion of the country's population and show considerable contrasts among themselves. First, and most fundamental, is the contrast between the plains of newer and older alluvium. The latter has been uplifted or is being incised by rivers starting a new cycle of erosion; it is difficult to irrigate and the soils are often coarse and heavily leached. The former, the newer alluvium, is by contrast both fertile and easy to irrigate. Secondly, there is the contrast in size between the mountain-rimmed pockets of plain along the Annam coast strip and the extensive, partly deltaic, lowlands of Tonkin and Cochin China. The most closely and anciently settled of these is the Red River lowland of Tonkin. This is a structural trough filled by sediments in recent geological times and still being veneered by alluvium from the Red River. It is in some ways the most favoured of all the lowlands for it gets rain from both the summer and winter monsoons so that year-round cropping is possible. The Red River, however, is a turbulent and difficult river, with very high waters in late summer and only the elaboration of a complex irrigation technology, involving the construction of massive dykes and embankments, has made it possible for the lower lands to be cropped in safety. The area of the Mekong Delta is an area of much lighter and more recent settlement. The richest soils are those developed on the young alluvium along the Mekong; away from the river as in central Cochin China and west of Saigon the 'gray soils' are developed on the more heavily leached older alluvium. And considerable areas remain in a poorly-drained marshy condition. If one seeks the explanation for the contrasts in intensity of settlement and land use between Tonkin and Cochin China we must seek it, not so much in terms of the soil factor, for many of the soils of the Tonkin delta are relatively poor, but in terms of the superior hydraulic techniques of the North Vietnamese and the long centuries of human occupance which have gradually built up the level of soil fertility.

The lowlands of Indonesia are extensive but of very uneven value. That of North Sumatra, for example, extends from northwest to southeast for some 850 miles and attains a width

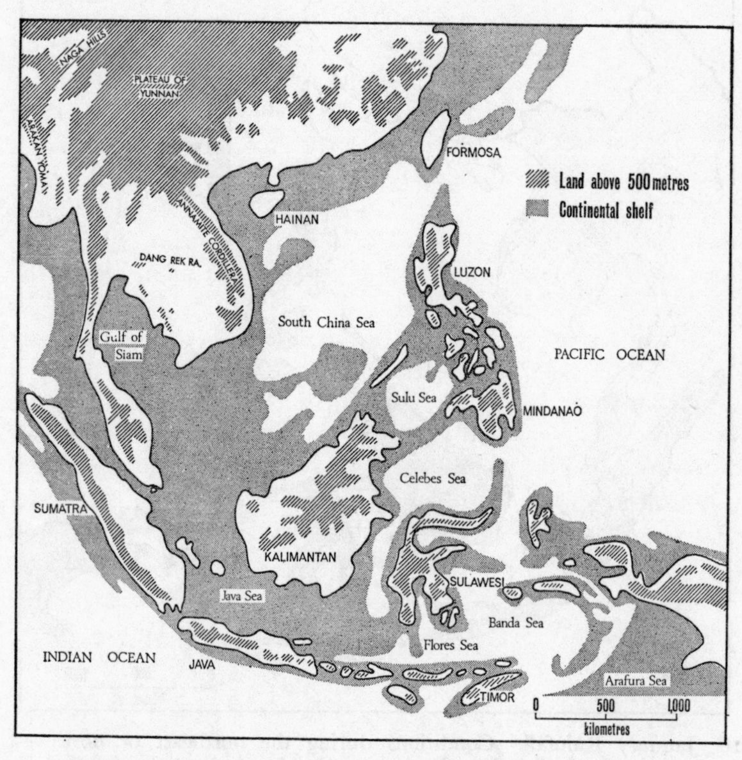

15 The Major Elements in Southeast Asia's Relief. The mountains, forming the frayed-out margins of Eurasia; the lowlands, of uneven agricultural value; and the shallow seas of the continental shelf.

of 150 miles in the south. Much of it consists of featureless swamp underlain by great thicknesses of peat and traversed by meandering rivers subject to unmanageable floods. The major exception is in the northeast, where the plain is much narrower and here the soils are much more fertile, being derived from the volcanic rocks of the Batak district; this northeastern area is the

Cultuurgebied, the plantation zone, of Dutch Sumatra. The lowlands of Java are much narrower and form a long corridor, some 10–20 miles wide, whose alluvial soils are replenished by volcanic ejecta. Where these volcanic materials are neutral

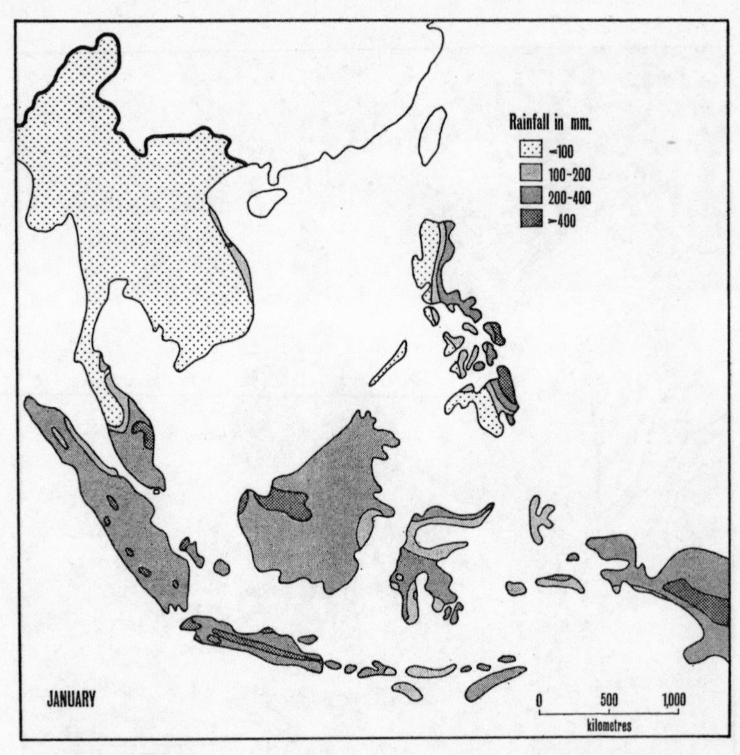

16 January Rainfall. Conditions during the northeast or northwest monsoon; relative drought over most of mainland Southeast Asia, except Annam coast strip; rainfall relatively heavy on windward slopes, e.g. eastern margins of Philippines.

or basic the soils have a high fertility; in the west, however, acidic materials predominate and soils are much less fertile and the density of population lower. Borneo repeats some of the features of Sumatra; the coastal lowlands are wide and swampy and the rivers which traverse them are subject to erratic régimes and it is the resulting difficulty of access, no less than the dense forest and the impoverished lateritic soils of the interior, that has been responsible for the island's belated development. And farther to the east, in islands such as Celebes (Sulawesi), the two zones of Tertiary folding described earlier intersect; there has been extensive faulting,

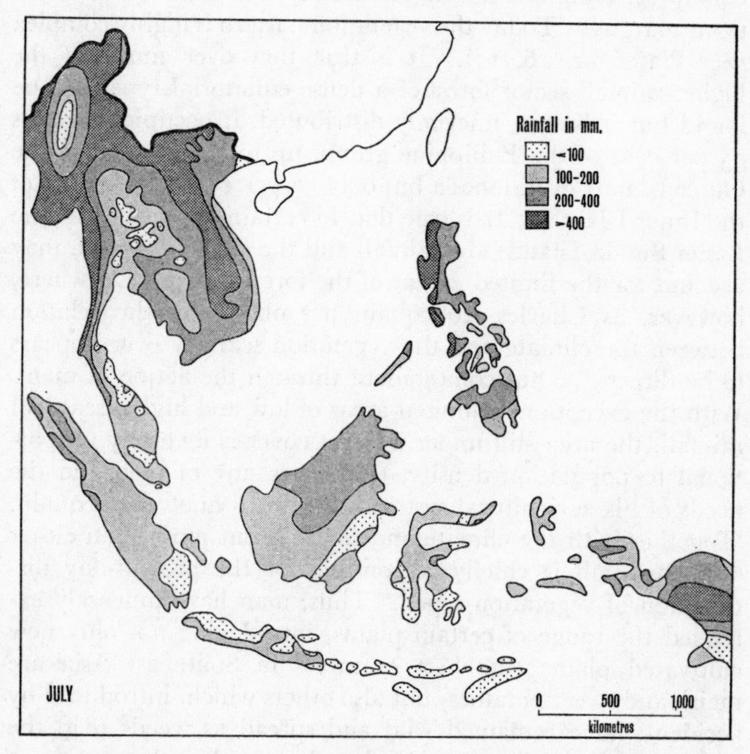

17 July Rainfall. Summer monsoon conditions bringing maximum of rain to most of mainland Southeast Asia and western Philippines; note rain-shadow areas of central Burma and central Thailand.

uplift and subsidence and the narrow coastal lowlands offer only limited opportunities to the agriculturalist.

The vegetation pattern summates the influence of physiographic and climatic conditions and also the biotic impact in the shape of human interference by clearing and burning. The region is characterised by a great variety of plant species and at an earlier period appears to have been largely dominated by high forest; this latter was either of the true rain-forest type or of a more open deciduous (or monsoon) type, the boundary between these two formations following, but only in a very general fashion, the boundary between the constantly wet equatorial climate and the seasonally-wet climates on their polar margins. Today the vegetation pattern is highly complex (See Plates 12, 16, 17). It is true that over much of the higher-rainfall sector forest of a dense equatorial type is to be found but it is very unevenly distributed; it occupies perhaps 55 per cent of the Philippine group, up to 70 per cent of the Outer Islands of Indonesia but only 30 per cent of the area of the Inner Islands. It is true that in certain areas, such as the Lesser Sunda Islands low rainfall and the long dry season may account for the limited extent of the forest cover. Elsewhere, however, as Charles Robequain has observed, 'the relation between the climate and the vegetation scarcely ever appears to be direct . . . but comes about through the action of man'. With the exception of limited areas of low and highly seasonal rainfall, the area still under a forest cover is inversely proportional to population density, to the pressure of man and the needs of his agricultural system. Again to quote Robequain, 'Together with the climate and the soil, but more than either of them, man is chiefly responsible for the present-day distribution of vegetation-types'. Thus, man has immensely extended the range of certain plants, introducing not only new cultivated plants (the best examples in Southeast Asia are maize and sweet potatoes) but also others which, introduced by accident, have remained wild and spread as weeds (e.g. the shrub *Lantana* in Timor). He has destroyed in the process of clearing for cultivation vast areas of forest, which is replaced by secondary formations and, in extreme cases, by grass savannas which cover some 20–30 per cent of Indonesia and over 40 per cent of the Philippines. This 'savannisation' certainly began before the coming of the European but it has accelerated in recent years as a result of growing population pressure and the extension and intensification of traditional cultivating and collecting economies.

This process should be stressed for it draws our attention to the fact that over a considerable area of Southeast Asia the vegetation is a 'man-made' vegetation (a 'biotic climax') rather than a 'natural' vegetation. Over much of lowland Southeast Asia man has substituted for the original swamp or

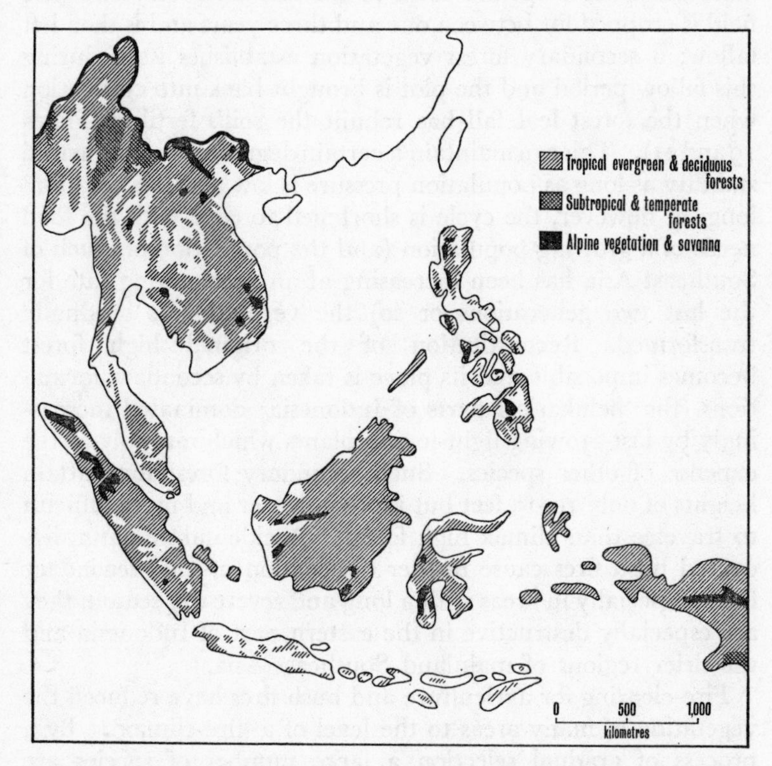

18 Generalised Vegetation Map. A forest mantle of varying density covers much of the area. This has been locally much modified by human clearing and cutting and is broken by discontinuous zones of more open country dominated by man's crops (notably rice), by swamps or by man-created grasslands.

forest a cover of cultivated plants, chiefly various types of rice, whose existence is dependent on human action such as irrigation, drainage and the suppression of competing weeds. In such areas, and parts of the Red River delta are an example, the natural vegetation has been eliminated. Outside these areas, and especially in upland Southeast Asia, the basic system of farming is one of shifting cultivation or swidden agriculture. Under this system the natural vegetation is cut, burned at the end of the dry season, and after a perfunctory cultivation the crops are sown in the ash-enriched soil. The field is cropped for between one and three years and is then left fallow; a secondary forest vegetation establishes itself during this fallow period and the plot is brought back into cultivation when the forest leaf fall has rebuilt the soil's fertility (Plates 19 and 21). This can maintain a certain degree of environmental stability as long as population pressure is low and the 'rotation' long; if, however, the cycle is shortened to cope with the food needs of a growing population (and the population of much of Southeast Asia has been increasing at an accelerating rate for the last two generations or so) the vegetation is gradually transformed. Reconstitution of the original high forest becomes impossible and its place is taken by secondary formations (the 'belukar' of parts of Indonesia) dominated increasingly by fast-growing light-loving plants which multiply at the expense of other species. Such secondary forest may attain heights of only 10–15 feet but is often denser and more difficult to traverse than climax high forest. Accidental or naturally-caused bush fires cause further destruction of such secondary forest especially in areas with a long and severe dry season; they are especially destructive in the eastern part of Indonesia and the drier regions of mainland Southeast Asia.

Fire-clearing for agriculture and bush fires have reduced the vegetation of many areas to the level of a 'fire-climax'. By a process of gradual selection a large number of species are eliminated and those that are fire-tolerant survive, adapting themselves to the changing conditions. There is a general impoverishment of the vegetation (in terms of number of species) and there develops a vegetation consisting of large areas of more or less homogeneous open forest diversified by patches of tree-dotted grassland very different from the original high forest. The transition from primary high forest through secondary woodland to savanna is gradual; the regional variety of vegetation is thus very great. However, the outcome of repeated burning is always the same—the creation of a savanna dominated by tall grasses and perpetuated by annual grass fires. In some areas, as in east Java, these savannas are dotted with fan palms (giving an African-type landscape); in extreme cases they are interspersed with succulents such as prickly pear or euphorbia. This replacement of a moisture-loving (hygrophilous) forest climax by a drought-tolerant (xerophytic) vegetation is an index to the extent to which man has transformed his original environment.

Climatic conditions, coupled with low level of living, favour a great luxuriance of diseases and in this respect Southeast Asia is very similar to tropical Africa. Some of these diseases, such as the smallpox which regularly ravaged the Indies, have been brought increasingly under contol. Others are 'social diseases' and their control is heavily dependent on improved living standards; an example is tuberculosis whose high rate of incidence in some of the bigger cities is a reflection of poor housing conditions. The major endemic disease is, however, malaria and this shows a highly complex pattern as a result of the very definite ecological preferences of the various types of *Anopheles* mosquito which are its vector. Paradoxically, the seasonally-flooded rice-growing lowlands of Southeast Asia are not major foci of the disease though *Anopheles aconitus* is responsible for outbreaks of malaria in east Java and *Anopheles ludlowii*, breeding in fishponds and in brackish sun-lit lagoon waters, is another lowland vector. It is, however, in the hill areas that malaria attains its greatest importance and it was the menace of malaria which was largely responsible for the evil reputation of the uplands among the more advanced peoples of Southeast Asia and for the scanty settlement of these areas. And the clearing of such areas for European plantation production (e.g. rubber in the Annamite cordillera) was responsible for major epidemics of malaria; in such cases the vector was *Anopheles maculatus* which breeds of preference in clear, sunlit, running water and for which the opening-up of the vegetation provided more favourable conditions of habitat. The influence of these differing preferences on the part of the malaria vector on the pattern of human settlement is illustrated clearly in the case of Borneo where the coast plains are relatively free from malaria and where the major zone of *Anopheles* concentration is the low foothill country; here the major concentrations of population are either on the coastal plain or on the uplands above the malarial zone. The use of prophylactics such as quinine or paludrine may give a high degree of immunity and measures such as the screening of houses and the treating of standing water with oil may reduce the danger of infection. The surest way to control the disease, however, lies in breaking the man-mosquito-hematozoa complex by eradicating the mosquito. D.D.T. may achieve a measure of control, though D.D.T.-resistant strains of mosquito may negate the initial achievement and a more successful long-term approach would seem to lie in the modification of the environment to create ecological conditions unfavourable to the mosquito. This, in turn, depends on detailed entomological work to establish the type and ecological requirements of the malaria vector in each area. And, as in most tropical areas, there is a wide range of other diseases which, if not killing diseases, contribute to lower the efficiency and reduce the expectation of life of Southeast Asia's peoples. These include the dysenteries, both amoebic and bacillary, various types of worm diseases, a wide range of deficiency diseases (whose impact is reflected in high child mortality rates) and epidemic diseases such as cholera in the crowded areas of the mainland or scrub typhus.

It is partly the influence of these diseases, rather than the direct influence of climate itself, which accounts for the 'tropical lethargy' commented on by some writers and for the relatively low expectation of life. Tropical disease is an essential element in what Ritchie Calder has aptly termed the 'misery-go-round of poverty'; the peasant suffers from malaria or some other tropical disease, illness makes him an inefficient farmer so that his crop yields are low and he is imperfectly nourished—and because he is poorly nourished he is particularly vulnerable to disease. And one point may be stressed here, for it is of fundamental importance in many of these Southeast Asian countries which are moving towards a re-structuring of their society, and that is that the vulnerability of human groups to these various pathogenic complexes—whether insect-transmitted as in the case of malaria or parasitic as in the case of hookworm—depends largely on the level of social and economic organisation. An organised society possessing the resources and technical skills can successfully withstand these diseases (e.g. the white settler groups in the tropics) and disease becomes important as a limiting factor only in the case of weak and technologically-backward societies.

CHAPTER 4

The Food-getting Economies of Southeast Asia

THE LINK between the physical environment, whose broad lines are sketched in Figures 13–18 and in the preceding section, and man is represented by man's food-getting economies; these provide the framework within which the various human groups appraise and turn to their own purposes the potentialities of the environment. The character of this exploitation and thus the meaning of the environment to any group is a function of the culture of that group; to a group possessing a relatively undeveloped technology a given environment will offer a relatively limited range of resources (e.g. the food-collecting peoples of interior Malaya or the upland Philippines depend on the game resources and wild fruits offered by the rain-forest); with each development in technology the meaning of the environment changes and the range of resources which can be utilised becomes wider. Life becomes more secure and the economy more diversified—and a diversified economy, like a house with several stories, can accommodate many more people than an undiversified, single-storey, type of economy.

Today, Southeast Asia shows a wide range of economies—at the one extreme, food-gathering and collecting of the simplest type, at the other the complex and sophisticated urban-industrial economies developed in the great cities. And between these two extremes is found a broad spectrum of agricultural economies—shifting cultivation, sedentary cultivation on 'dry' fields, sedentary cultivation based upon highly developed irrigation techniques. With each of these techniques is associated a particular form of social organisation and a particular level of population density; it is, as we shall see, largely in terms of these that the distribution of population must be explained.

The earliest peoples to occupy the area were alithic or pre-paleolithic food-gatherers, hunters and fishers, folk who had not made the transition to a stone-using culture. Today remnants of these occur over a widely extended arc from mainland Southeast Asia to the islands. Their units of social organisation are small, often the hunting-group or the clan, and they are nomadic in habit, yet moving within a clearly defined hunting territory. Typically, there is a division of labour between the sexes, the men hunting while the women and children collect vegetable foods and insects. Though such groups are labelled 'primitive' they have, nevertheless, developed elaborate techniques for utilising poisonous vegetable substances and for the preserving of foodstuffs. And in some of their practices we can glimpse the beginnings of agriculture: the Semang of Malaya, for example, will clear the ground round a fruit-bearing durian—a rudimentary form of tree cultivation—and put back into the ground the tops of wild yams so that they may produce new tubers.

In his discussion of the transition to agriculture the German writer Hahn distinguished between primitive agriculture or hoe-tillage, whose development he ascribes to women, and advanced or plough agriculture. It is not easy to apply this generalised distinction to Southeast Asia, for many groups use neither hoe nor plough but the digging stick while other groups practise advanced sedentary agriculture with the hoe as the basic implement. 'Advanced' agriculture in the area does not thus depend on the animal-drawn plough, nor 'primitive' agriculture on the hoe. Karl Pelzer has suggested that the most fundamental distinction between advanced and primitive agriculture is to be found less in the tools used than in the land use pattern. Primitive agriculture, he points out, is characterised by small ragged stump-littered clearings scattered through the forest; advanced sedentary tillage by the well-tended permanently cultivated plot, manured and intensively worked, often terraced and irrigated. 'Shifting cultivation and sedentary cultivation', he says, 'are generic terms used to describe fundamental differences in land use, differences that find their outward expression in the cultural landscapes created by those who maintain these economies.' The extreme representatives of these two systems are, on one hand, the tiny fire-cleared plots of the hill tribes of the Annamite Cordillera, on the other, the meticulously-cultivated and skilfully-dyked paddy landscapes of, say, the Red River lowland or the plains of Java. Today, these two systems are complementary in their distribution, advanced agriculture (in its various forms) being characteristic of the lowland areas, and especially the alluvial lowlands; primitive agriculture, by contrast has been pushed, as a result of the expansion of more vigorous people practising a more advanced agriculture, to the marginal areas—the upland zones of mainland Southeast Asia and the forested interiors of the larger islands such as Borneo. There are also racial contrasts between the groups practising the two systems, for those who practice the more primitive types of agriculture belong to some of the earlier stocks—negrito, Nesiot and the like—who originally occupied much of the region but who have been displaced by later groups.

The food-getting economies of Southeast Asia can be classified, on the basis of the techniques employed, into the following types:

1. Shifting Cultivation
2. Sedentary Agriculture
   (*a*) Wet rice cultivation
   (*b*) Garden cultivation
   (*c*) Dry field cultivation

The main features of each system may be sketched in briefly.

SHIFTING CULTIVATION

The shifting cultivators of Southeast Asia—and some of the tribes of upland Vietnam are excellent examples—have inserted themselves into the existing ecological equilibrium (the climate-vegetation-soil complex), creating for themselves a 'living-space' with the minimum disruption of that equilibrium; incapable of mastering nature, theirs has been a *passive adjustment* to the environment quite different from the domination of the environment typified by the rice-growing economy of Tonkin. In generalised terms, these groups are at an Iron Age level of culture, possessing weaving, pottery, basket-making and iron. They did not, however, reach the level reached by the Iron Age peasants of Western Europe in the eighteenth century, the level characterised by a stable agricultural system based on fallowing. Instead, they base their agriculture on a system of forest/field rotation which makes it possible to utilise the forest in such a fashion that the tree cover can regenerate and protect and renew the fragile and vulnerable tropical soil. Fire, in the shape of controlled burning of the forest to clear their plots, is perhaps their most important 'tool'; the crop is grown in the ash-fertilised soil of the fire-cleared field, cultivation is of the simplest and when, after a year or so, the level of fertility of the soil declines the field is abandoned and a fresh clearing is made. Meanwhile, the forest invades the abandoned plot and the forest leaf-fall gradually builds up the fertility, and above all the humus content of the depleted soil. The system is thus one of rotation of fields rather than rotation of crops; it is a system dependent on the forest cover to maintain fertility; it is a system whose success depends on the maintenance of the soil/vegetation equilibrium. And ultimately it is a system which depends on a low man/land ratio, for increasing population pressure means an increasing area under crops and this can be achieved only at the cost of the soil-restoring fallow period—and if this is cut short the forest fails to regenerate and a downward spiral of deterioration, and eventually destruction, of the environment begins. Some indication of the extent to which the system sets an upper limit to population density is given by Van Beukering's estimate—that a typical shifting cultivator and his family occupy some $2\frac{1}{2}$ acres of land a year; this, assuming a family unit of five and nine years fallow for every year under crops, would give a maximum density of 130 people per square mile (this assumes that *all* the area is suitable to cultivation when in actual fact only one-half or less may be cultivable—which means a correspondingly reduced overall population density). It is the low population-carrying capacity of the system, coupled with the fact that the peoples of East Asia have never developed the techniques of livestock management which would enable them to utilise their upland regions, that explains the thinly-settled character of much of Southeast Asia (Figure 22).

SEDENTARY AGRICULTURE

Economically and socially the transition from shifting to sedentary agriculture represents a major step forward because sedentary cropping, giving higher and more certain yields, permits the beginning of that accumulation of surplus on which the economic and social diversification of the community's life depend. The sedentary agricultural communities are, in consequence, a good deal more complex than the communities of shifting cultivators; non-agricultural activities such as the handicraft industries are often well developed (with some measure of local specialisation, giving rise to inter-village trade) and the fabric of local administration, usually on a village basis, is much more strongly organised. The various types of sedentary agriculture—wet-rice cultivation, garden cultivation and dry-field cultivation—are often closely associated; nevertheless, there are practical advantages in considering each separately.

(*a*) *Wet-Rice Cultivation* This occupies a distinctive 'ecological niche' in Southeast Asia, the type of environment termed by Spencer 'the moist aquatic fringe'. It is typical of the major alluvial lowlands of the region, from the lowland of the Red River in the north to the coast plains of Java and Celebes in the south. It is the most distinctive type of agriculture in the region; indeed, the very term 'Southeast Asia' conjures up a vision of close-settled carefully tended *sawahs* (irrigated rice-fields) against a backdrop of palms or forested hills. Yet in spite of the very wide extension of the system today we do well to bear in mind C. A. Fisher's demonstration that its adoption dates often from a relatively recent period in the region's history. It had certainly established itself at an early date in areas such as Tonkin, adjacent to its Chinese centre of origin, and it appears at a relatively early date in central and east Java. But in Malaya its introduction dates from the period of Indian acculturation; in Indochina the Khmer state as late as the fifteenth century appears to have depended on both irrigated rice cultivation in the vicinity of Angkor *and* on shifting cultivation; in west Java it was adopted after the Europeans had appeared on the scene. And this relatively late expansion into certain areas is to be explained less in environmental terms (i.e. the absence of land suited to this type of agriculture) than in social and cultural terms, for wet-rice cultivation (and especially where based on river-fed irrigation systems) called for a high degree of technical skill and on a developed and stable system of local government able to ensure the effective control and distribution of water resources. Whether the decisive factor in the spread of this type of agriculture was an increasing population which forced man to make those changes in his society in which the system of irrigated rice-growing was possible, or whether it was the adoption of this system after a period of social and political consolidation which was responsible for the high densities of population associated with this system we shall probably never know.

Today, in the peasant areas of the mainland, the terms 'sedentary agriculture' and 'rice cultivation' are virtually synonymous; in Cambodia, for example, nine-tenths of the cropland is under rice. Only locally, as in the eastern islands of Indonesia, where maize and sago become important staples, is this dominance challenged. Long centuries of trial and error have made possible the development of literally thousands of varieties of rice with differing lengths of growing season (ranging from two to ten months) and a wide range of tolerance as far as soil and water conditions are concerned; some of the so-called 'floating rices' will grow in flood waters up to 10 feet deep, other rices have a high tolerance of salinity and are thus adapted to the coastal margins of the great deltas. Irrigation techniques are less evenly developed. There is a basic contrast between the rain-fed irrigation of parts of Cambodia and the river-fed irrigation systems of the Vietnamese lands. There are, moreover, wide contrasts in the degree of technical skill shown by those groups who practise irrigation from river waters; indeed, perhaps the only group to achieve a complete mastery of the water resources of an area are the

Vietnamese of the Red River lowland whose agriculture depends on a complex and sophisticated system of dyking which has effectively controlled a river notorious for its turbulence and rapid rise during the monsoon period. This mastery was, however, achieved relatively late in Vietnamese history. Other groups, such as the Thai or the Burmese, show no such competence in the field of irrigation; yet other groups, as in the Philippines, are using highly developed systems of terracing and irrigation inherited from an earlier period. And to this diversity must be added the diversity arising from historical circumstances, notably the fact that some areas, such as the Mekong Delta and parts of Lower Burma, were occupied by rice-growing peoples relatively recently; they were indeed 'pioneer fringes' until the late nineteenth century, and their lower density of population reflects the recency of their occupation by man.

It may be noted that terracing solves the problem of erosion but that the wet-rice cultivator is still faced with the problem of maintaining fertility. This is less important in areas such as Java where the irrigation water contains silt derived from recent volcanic rocks but elsewhere complex systems of crop rotation and green manuring play an important role in maintaining the soil nutrient status; an example is the cropping of *sawahs* with leguminous crops during the dry season in Java. The contribution of the various types of algae that flourish in the waters of the flooded ricefield may be significant; however, as yet it is only partially investigated.

(*b*) *Garden Cultivation* This many-storied type of cultivation, integrating bananas and tree crops with a wide range of vegetable crops, is regarded by some as the remnant of a primitive grainless hoe culture formerly much more widely distributed in Southeast Asia. It is above all concerned with the production of those crops not needed in large quantities but used to supplement the diet and add flavour to the basic meal of rice. It is a type of cultivation that is well developed in Java (where it locally occupies up to 15 per cent of the agricultural area) and in parts of Siam; it is developed on the sandy river terrace soils along the Mekong in Cambodia (where it is known as *chamcar* cultivation) and on the sandy terrace soils of South Vietnam. Its distribution is a reflection not only of ecological conditions but also of social conditions for, as has been observed in Siam and South Vietnam, it is only where the peasant has security of tenure that he has any incentive to plant fruit trees and to undertake intensive garden-type cultivation.

(*c*) *Dry-Field Cultivation* Two trends may be seen in historical development of dry-field cultivation especially in the Indonesian area. Firstly, the tendency for rice cultivation 'to spread beyond areas of agricultural terracing and water control', to become a crop produced under dry-field, or even shifting agricultural techniques. Secondly, with the advent of the European and the attempts to encourage 'sedentarisation', there was an increasing emphasis on permanent cultivation. This, coupled with the increasing world demand for tropical crops and the rising local demand for food crops, led to a marked expansion of dry-field (*tegalan*) cultivation. This trend has been less evident on the mainland than in the Indies; here the spread of dry-field cultivation has, as in Madura, led to extensive deforestation and erosion. This, indeed, is one of the main drawbacks of dry-field as opposed to wet-field cultivation for even in moderately, dissected country it is wasteful of soil resources and offers no real long-term stability. The basic problem faced by the cultivator is that of maintaining fertility and it is a problem much more acute than that faced by the *sawah* cultivator. Livestock manure is used when available, as is rotational cropping and, above all, the use of green manure crops. These latter, however, have one major drawback and that is that they are unsuited to areas of high population density where the peasant cannot spare the land for a non-food crop; it is nevertheless precisely in such areas that the drain on soil nutrients is greatest and the need for some form of manuring the greatest.

CROPPING SYSTEMS

So far, the discussion has been limited to the major *land use systems* represented in the region; little has been said about the *basic crop assemblages*, those 'biological auxiliaries' on which man has based his life and his well-being. Two major assemblages are involved, first, what J. E. Spencer has termed 'the yam-taro-sago cropping complex', secondly, the rice complex, with its agricultural terracing and developed control of water

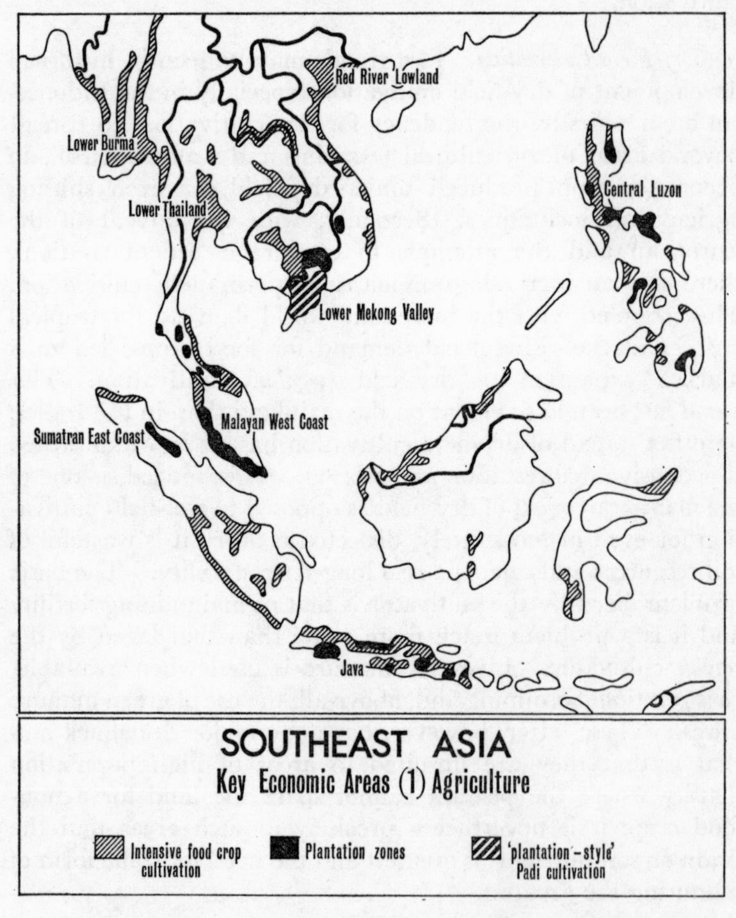

19 Key Economic Areas: Agriculture. Extremely patchy pattern of development, with concentration in the rice-growing lowlands; major areas of plantation development (e.g. rubber in Malaya and the Indochinese lands are shown) together with the 'plantation-style' rice economy of the relatively recently-settled lands of Cochin China.

supplies. The relationships between these two systems can be better appreciated if set in a historical context.

Carl Sauer has suggested that the cradle area of early agriculture lay in Southeast Asia, more precisely in the Bay of Bengal coastlands comprising Burma, the adjoining areas of Siam and Indochina, and parts of the coast plain of eastern India. This area, he says, 'meets the requirements of high physical and organic diversity, of mild climates with . . . abundant rainy and dry periods, of many waters inviting to fishing, of location at the hub of the Old World for communication by water or by land. No other area is equally well suited or equally well furnished for the rise of a fishing farming culture.' It is to this area, he suggests, that we must look for the origin of farming (initially closely associated with fishing), for the beginnings of the domestication of animals, for the development of planting techniques and for the improvement of plants by vegetative reproduction.

It seems likely that this early development of agriculture was based on *planting*, on the production of crops from root stocks, stems or tubers. Selection proceeds by choosing the individual plant to be divided in order to establish a number of plants that are like the parent and by observing and preserving desirable variants. There is little attention to seeds and in some cases these cultivated plants have lost the capacity to bear seeds and are dependent on man for their continued survival. The list of these man-made plants or *cultigens* is large and many have been developed in the vicinity of the Bay of Bengal. They include the bananas, ginger, taro and the various yams which have been dispersed through the Pacific; certain palms such as sago; sugar; and breadfruit, citrus and other fruits. Of these, the most important have been the carbohydrate-producers—yams, taro and sago—which formed the basic food crop complex of Southeast Asia. These crops do not in themselves provide a balanced diet for they provide little protein; if, however, the thesis that this early agriculture was developed from a fishing culture is correct these protein needs would have been supplied by fish and shell-fish.

Alongside this domestication of plants domestication of animals also took place. The dog, the pig, the fowl, the duck

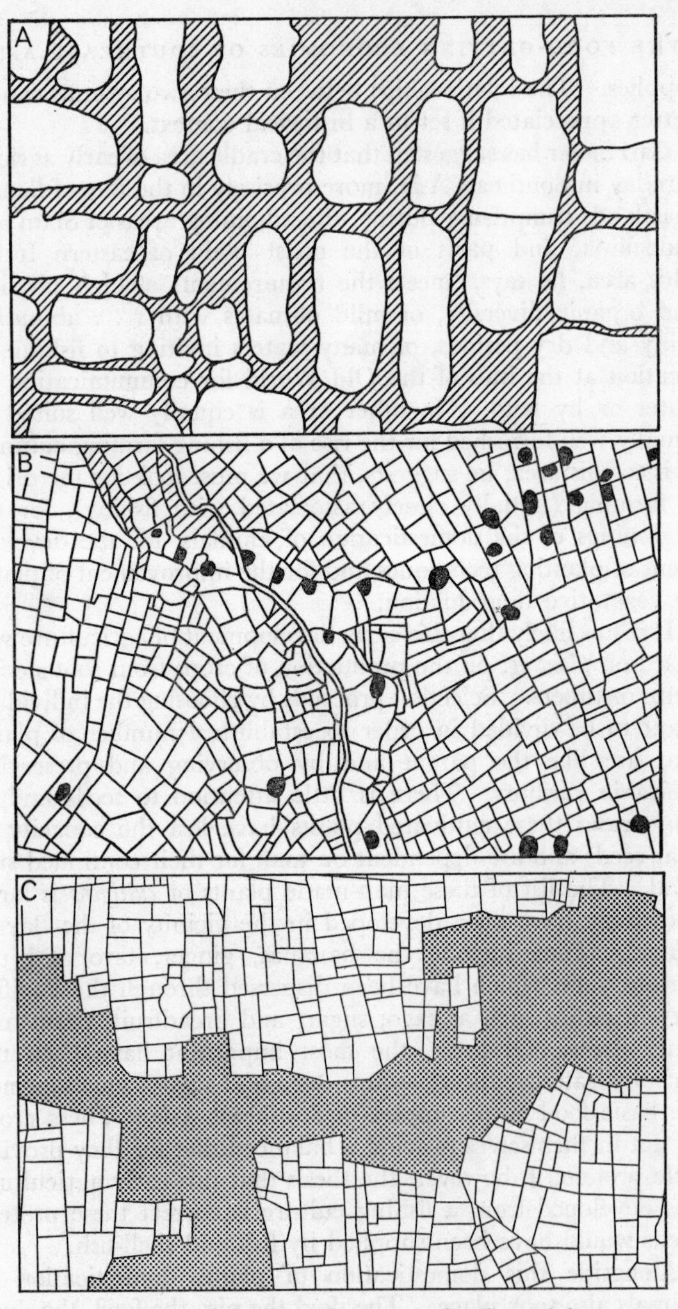

20 Contrasts in Field Patterns in Southeast Asia.

A. Cambodia: low man–land ratio reflected in large irregular fields set in matrix of bush.

B. Tonkin: extreme parcellation suggests heavy pressure of population.

C. Java: close association of *Sawah* and garden cultivation (stipple indicates settlements and gardens).

and the goose were all domesticated in Southeast Asia; they are essentially animals of the household, or farmyard, in contrast to the herd animals domesticated in southwest Asia.

At the earliest stage of settled agriculture in the region, then, man was dependent on the yam-taro-sago complex of plants, with domesticated animals of local origin and fishing to provide his protein needs. The subsequent agricultural history of the area centres around the progressive 'rolling-back' of the northwestern frontier of this early crop-complex as a result of the advance of the rice-complex. Spencer has sketched in the broad lines of this agricultural revolution. He sees the domestication of rice and the definition of dry-field and wet-field rice cultivation taking place somewhat over three millennia ago in 'upper mainland Southeast Asia', i.e. the Indochinese lands. The later introduction, in this region, of agricultural terracing 'permitted the evolution of a more productive wet-field system, practised on slopes above the flood plains, with an associated water-control system'. It was this rice-complex which was carried southwards from its original cradle area by groups who migrated to various parts of the mainland and islands of Southeast Asia, and who established a series of 'enclaves' of the new economy in ecologically-favourable areas within the yam-taro-sago agricultural realm. From these core areas, which included, for example, Java, rice cultivation spread out, often beyond the areas where terracing and water control were possible and often reverting under these conditions to dry-field types of cultivation. The pattern of diffusion of the new economy and the new crop was uneven: for example, parts of Java had developed a relatively sophisticated *sawah* economy by the sixteenth century but rice may not have entered Malaya until the thirteenth or fourteenth century and as late as the fifteenth century sago and fruits are described as primary local foods in Malacca. In addition, environmental factors, notably the problem of acclimatising rice strains and the difficulty of developing adequate water-control schemes, limited the expansion of the rice complex east of Java. The general picture which emerges is one of a progressive but uneven retreat of the earlier yam-taro-sago complex in the face of the newer wet-rice complex. The beginning of this retreat dates back far into the early history of the region but because of the ecological problems involved the processes by which the earlier cropping system were replaced were extremely slow. In consequence, as Spencer has observed 'the geographical distribution of cropping systems today is a relatively recent maturing of processes originating many centuries ago'. And in some areas, as in the Philippines, Malaya or eastern Indonesia, this recency means that the rice economies of the area are 'not yet really mature or fully productive'.

CHAPTER 5

Social Geography and the Quality of Peasant Life

THERE IS, as we shall see later, a fundamental contrast in population conditions between the upland areas of South-east Asia and the lowlands. The former are thinly peopled (mean density is under 25 per square mile) while the latter contain some of the closely settled areas on the earth's surface. These remarkable densities of population in lowland Southeast Asia are based, not, as in the Atlantic world, on industry but on intensive exploitation of the soil by peasant families, living on tiny plots of land. In prewar Tonkin, for example, the average size of holding was between one and two acres; in Java approximately one acre. Traditionally the land belonged to the cultivator but in many areas, as a result of population pressure in the delta lands of the Red River or as the result of a process of land reclamation followed by the creation of large estates as in the Mekong delta region, there emerged a class of what Pierre Gourou terms 'proletarian owners', peasants whose plot is completely inadequate to support them at a reasonable level of living. In contrast to, say, Black Africa, land attachment is strong and these peasant groups are 'earth-bound societies'. This is partly due to religious factors, partly, according to some investigators, to the rice-based character of the economy—for rice, as a crop, is not only demanding in terms of environmental conditions and thus encourages a marked localisation of population, it also gives a high output of food per unit area and thus is a 'factor of density'. And as additional factors contributing to this concentration of 'many men on little land' in the past we may add resignation, a centuries-old resignation to a marginal existence and the traditional religious attachment to the ideal of a large family.

Each of these concentrations of population can be broken down into an infinite number of villages, tiny social and economic 'cells'; it is this cell-like structure which gives Southeast Asia's civilisations their strength and their resilience. And this was nowhere better illustrated than in Vietnam at the time of the First Indochinese War when the French held all the keypoints and a crushing superiority in weapons and society was reduced to a network of villages—yet, because these villages 'held', Vietnamese society and the Vietnamese nation endured and emerged. These villages are both political and economic centres; village political life is strongly democratic, governed by a traditional law which has often outlasted the codes of law superimposed by a central government and in the administration of the village all the family heads are equal, any special consideration being due to age or personal merits. Where the economy is based on irrigation the exploitation of irrigated land calls for a strong solidarity among the villagers and develops habits of collective administration and self-dependence. And, in turn, each village consists of a multitude of smaller 'cells', the family units. These are families in the restricted sense of the term, consisting of the father, mother and children—in all, some 4–6 persons; the family is the basic social group and at the same time the basic economic group since in the traditional societies it was—and still is in those areas where socialisation of agriculture has not yet taken place—the basic unit in the system of land exploitation.

The civilisation of Southeast Asia is both vegetable and vegetarian, concerned with the production of food crops (with livestock products playing a very restricted role) and relying on human and animal muscle for power. Over much of the area the dominant type of stock is the water buffalo and numbers in relation to population are low (one beast to ten people or more) though the livestock density per unit of agricultural area may be as high as in the U.S.A. Pigs and poultry exist on village waste but the peasant is not a stock-rearer in any sense of the term, rather is he essentially and completely an agriculturalist. The farming system is *intensive* but this has a different meaning from that in the West. In Western farming high yields and high output per acre are achieved by the heavy application of fertilisers, by the use of machinery which makes it possible to reduce the costs of production—and in the use of both fertilisers and machinery the farmer is guided by the law of diminishing returns. But in Southeast Asia, as in East Asia, intensive farming is inspired by different motives: it aims at the largest possible output by multiplying harvests, if necessary at the cost of diminishing returns per harvest; with shortage of food always at his elbow the peasant must produce *regardless of cost.* Techniques are very highly developed but, as the transplanting of rice suggests, are extremely labour-consuming. Inter-planting of crops, practised under market-gardening conditions, is another example of refined techniques which are prodigal of labour; so, too, is the profound transformation of the soil through manuring, marling and deep cultivation. In such an economy there is little place for livestock-rearing for meat or milk; the food resources available for animals are limited for the lowlands are largely under crops, and techniques of upland utilisation by livestock grazing (as in Western Europe) scarcely exist. Moreover, the production of food for man through the medium of livestock is a wasteful process and where maximum output (in terms of calories per unit area) is essential animal rearing is perforce eliminated.

It is perhaps surprising, in view of the intensive character of the system, that its productivity is relatively low. Rice is supposed to be a high-yielding crop, yet Java's rice yield of 12 cwt. per acre was the same as France's wheat yield (and France's agriculture was by no means the most efficient and high-yielding in Europe). In Malaya and Indochina yields were even lower (10 cwt. per acre); for comparison, yields in Japan, which were the highest in Asia, were comparable with Danish wheat yields (27 cwt. per acre). There is no reason to suppose Japanese soils are inherently more productive than those of, say, Java and the explanation for these contrasting levels of productivity per unit-area must be sought in the higher level of technical efficiency of Japanese agriculture and, above all, in the much heavier use of fertilisers. This is of some importance for it means that a much higher level of output could be achieved—and with it a perceptible increase in the levels of peasant living—without any increase in area under cultivation. Such a *technical transformation* of peasant farming, which calls for an expanded output of fertilisers and of equipment such as better tools and irrigation pumps, is dependent on industrialisation in the region. And this in turn is dependent either on external aid (which may result in the creation of dependent economies) or on the mobilisation of hidden resources within the rural sector; these resources include that share of the crop 'skimmed off' by a largely parasitic landlord group and a labour force which is at present idle for a considerable proportion of the year. Such a mobilisation has been carried through by the Asian socialist régimes and, as their example illustrates, it can be achieved only if rural society (notably the land tenure and credit systems) is completely refashioned.

A second distinctive feature is the generally small and often fragmented character of the landholdings; only in areas of relatively recent settlement are there any marked exceptions. In southern and northeastern Thailand the average size of holdings is some 4 acres, in Java 1 acre, while in Tongking some three-fifths of all holdings were under 0·9 acres in size. Raymond Firth states that, under a system of *sawah* cultivation, a peasant household needs from 2½ to 5 acres for subsistence. In consequence, because of the small size of holding in many areas and in spite of double-cropping and extremely intensive land use, many families find themselves faced with the alternatives of seeking alternative work which will make possible the purchase of additional food or putting up with inadequate nutrition. 'Nothing is real to us but hunger' is an Asian saying—and the roots of this condition lie largely in the land tenure situation. The small size of farm holdings in the older-settled areas is largely a result of centuries of population growth and the problem it creates is aggravated by fragmentation; an individual holding may consist of several small plots widely scattered over the village area and, though this scattering may have some advantages (for example, it makes possible the inclusion within one holding of land with different soil and water conditions and it spreads the risk of pest damage), it nevertheless makes for difficulties in the use of labour and implements on an economic scale and for a significant wastage of land in the shape of dividing balks and paths. Consolidation and co-operative working of the land may obviate some of these problems but a real solution can come only with the economic diversification of the countryside which, by creating new avenues of employment in rural-located or urban industries, relieves the pressure of population on what is so often the only source of a livelihood—the land. As a corollary to this low level of productivity peasant incomes are low; in Java in the mid-twenties three-fifths of all families had incomes of less than £12 10*s*. 0*d*. a year while more recently Robert Ho has estimated the *per capita* income from rice-farming in Malaya at $(M)183 a year. In view of the necessity of obtaining cash to buy supplementary food before the harvest is ready or to meet such contingencies as weddings or funerals it is not surprising that the burden of peasant indebtedness is a problem; according to Ho three-quarters of all Malayan farmers are in debt.

It is sometimes tacitly assumed that the responsibility for poverty lies squarely on the shoulders of the peasant himself and those who hold such a view draw attention to the apparently considerable amount of wasted man-hours in the course of the agricultural year. Such a view overlooks two basic features of peasant life in the region. First, the unavoidable loss of working time due to diseases such as malaria or parasitic worm infestation to which the peasant's poverty makes him particularly vulnerable (and which, by reducing his efficiency as a worker, contribute to that poverty). Secondly, the highly seasonal character of the rice-growing economy, with its heavy labour demands at the time of transplanting and at harvest; so heavy are the demands at harvest time that even densely-populated areas may find they have no surplus labour. In areas with a highly seasonal rainfall régime and lacking the facilities for dry season irrigation the dry season is a period of enforced inactivity. It would seem therefore that one obvious solution to the problem of poverty lies in the development of economic activities which will absorb the labour of the 'dead season'; in the old days handicraft industries were important in this context but with the decline of these the need is to create alternative—and seasonal—non-agricultural employment as has been done in the Chinese countryside. And this is possible only if economic development is broadly based for both rural industrialisation and the electric pumps which will make possible year-round irrigation are largely dependent on rural electrification. Any real increase in peasant levels of living will thus demand a profound transformation of the countryside in the shape of structural change—i.e. changes in the land tenure system—and technical change. These will make possible a diversification of the rural economy and, as in China and increasingly in North Vietnam, will profoundly change the geography of the region.

It is often assumed that this peasant society was an extremely simple subsistence one but in part at least this assessment is of a society which had been partially disrupted by the impact of Europe. As Chesneaux has demonstrated in Vietnam, the countryside was characterised by a highly developed handicraft industry and within this industry a considerable measure of specialisation had grown up, with chains of villages engaged in the various stages of manufacturing goods (e.g. pottery). This economy possessed a complex marketing organisation, handling both local handicraft goods and agricultural produce and this industrial and commercial sector gave a measure of balance and stability to the rural life of many areas. Increasing imports of European manufacture precipitated the decline of the traditional handicraft industries and contributed to that 'agrarianisation' of rural life which is today regarded as one of the distinguishing features of an 'under-developed' region. At the same time, Western trading contacts and the growing Western demand for tropical products gave an increased significance to the purely commercial sector of the village economy. These developments resulted in a warping of the rural economy, a warping in which the decline of village industry was accompanied by an expansion of the tertiary and primary agricultural sectors, and in which the primary sector became increasingly 'polarised' between, on one hand, a subsistent food-getting economy and on the other a cash-getting economy dependent on distant markets whose workings the peasant did not understand and over which he had little control. The peasant discovered new needs, in the shape of western manufactured goods but, given the steady decline in the value of his primary products relative to that of manufactured goods, he finds these needs increasingly difficult to satisfy; there is, as Firth has observed, a 'widening gap between the peasants expanding range of wants and his level of productivity'. He becomes increasingly aware of this pauperisation and the general impoverishment of peasant life is aggravated by the steady build-up of population following the 'demographic revolution'.

CHAPTER 6

Political and Economic Integration with Europe

FOR MUCH of its history Southeast Asia has been oriented towards the two great culture-worlds of the Asian mainland—those of China and of India. This orientation was to be drastically changed as a result of the intrusion into the Far Eastern tropics of an expanding Europe, possessed of a superior military technology and seeking tropical produce and, from the nineteenth century onwards, a market for its manufactured goods. In mainland Southeast Asia the result of the European impact was to replace the former continental orientation of states such as Thailand or Annam with an oceanic orientation; throughout the whole area new political and economic links tied the Southeast Asian peoples into the politics and the economic needs of the European colonial powers.

This European intrusion, motivated in part at least by the desire to control the extremely lucrative spice trade, began in the early sixteenth century when the Portuguese seized Malacca (1511); this was the first of the series of trading posts which were to make up what has been termed the 'garrison empire' of the Portuguese. By the middle of the sixteenth century the Spanish, advancing from their Mexican colony across the Pacific, had begun to establish themselves in the Philippines; the capital of their new Southeast Asian empire—Manila—was founded in 1571. Dutch merchants, backed ultimately by Dutch sea-power, began to move into the region towards the end of the same century; the Dutch East India Company was founded in 1602. Britain and France entered on the scene a little later, Britain, through the agency of *her* East India Company, commencing the first hesitant commercial penetration of Burma and Siam in the early seventeenth century, while the French presence manifested itself in the shape of Catholic missionaries who commenced their labours in Siam and Tonkin in the latter half of the century. Initially, the European intruders were little concerned with territorial expansion, their main objective being to establish a chain of trading posts by means of which the wealth of Southeast Asia could be tapped. But inevitably, to protect the trading posts themselves and to stabilise conditions in their hinterlands so that commerce might flow unimpeded, the European powers were drawn into a process of territorial expansion, a process first manifested in Java. Then, as the relative value of the Asian coastal trade waned and as the emphasis of commerce shifted from the (high-value) spices to commodities such as sugar and coffee, an acceleration of this process of expansion was inevitable. Only under Western control could those measures, such as the Culture System (the compulsory cultivation of certain crops) of the Indies or the creation of plantation 'enclaves', necessary to ensure an uninterrupted and expanding flow of tropical products, be assured. During the second half of the nineteenth century this process of territorial expansion reached its peak and by the end of the century most of Southeast Asia had passed under the direct or indirect political control of Western European nations.

Other factors, too, played their part in drawing the European powers into a 'scramble for Southeast Asia'. In the case of Britain the desire to stabilise the eastern frontiers of India drew her into Burma; having established herself in Malaya, a similar desire to stabilise the northern frontier of Malaya led to the extension of British control over the four northern sultanates which had hitherto been under Siamese jurisdiction. In the case of both Britain and France the commercial prospects of tapping the wealth of China through rail-links to the south-western province of Yunnan (prospects never realised) explain in part the preoccupation of—and the rivalry between—these two great powers in the adjoining borderlands of Southeast Asia. And, as America became increasingly Asia-conscious, the United States saw in the crumbling Spanish empire in the

Philippines a valuable defensive bastion for her Pacific shore; the acquisition of these islands marks the first step in the creation of a defensive perimeter which today extends the

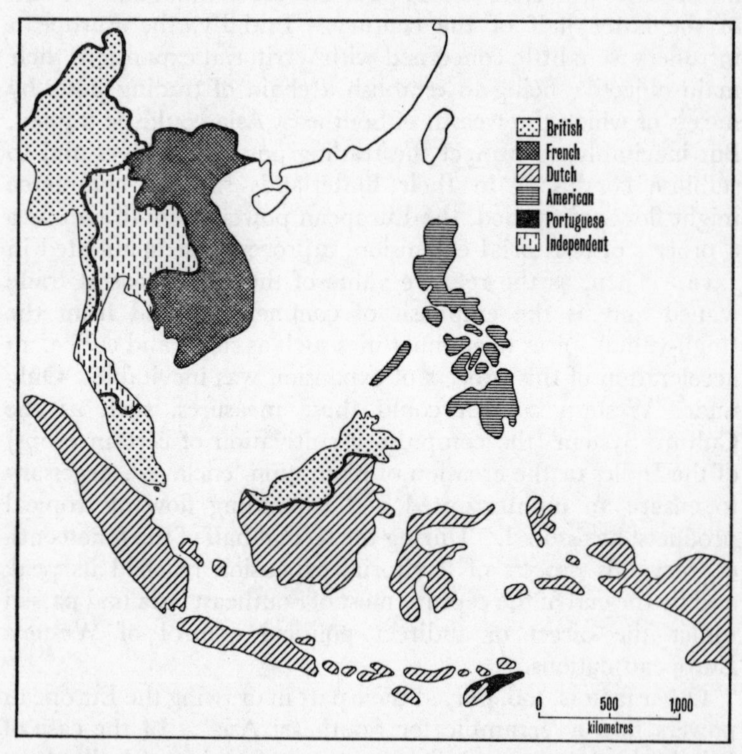

21 The Colonial Empires in Southeast Asia on the eve of the Second World War. Effective partition of the whole region, with exception of Siam, between the British, French, Dutch and Americans; relic of former Portuguese empire in eastern Timor.

length of the western Pacific, from Alaska through Japan and the formerly Japanese Pacific islands, to the Philippines.

One of the most obvious results of this was the fragmentation of pre-existing ethnic or national unities. The frontier between Siam and the French protectorate of Laos thus cut through the midst of a homogeneous Laotian Thai population. The boundary between the French colony of Cochin China and the protectorate of Cambodia was drawn in such a way that a sizeable Khmer population was cut off by the new boundaries from the majority of their fellow Khmers. The Malay-speaking world was partitioned between the Dutch who held the islands of Indonesia and the British who had established themselves in the Malayan peninsula (Penang 1786, Singapore 1819) and on the northern fringe of the Indonesian islands in Labuan.[1]

Political boundaries were redrawn, and the character of political power within the area changed. While a semblance of the traditional power structure was often preserved (e.g. the sultans in the Malayan and Indonesian territories, or the traditional rulers in the French protectorates of Annam, Cambodia or Laos) effective power was now in the hands of the administrators of the colonial power, and these were concerned with implementing the policies laid down in London, Paris or The Hague. And this administration functioned through its own bureaucracy, which often replaced the traditional *élites* and which was trained along Western lines. Over much of Southeast Asia this was the group from which the leaders and the administrators of the new nations were drawn when the colonial powers withdrew after the Second World War.

More important and more far-reaching in their effects than these political changes, however, were the economic changes. These took two forms. First, a re-orientation of the trade of much of the area, accompanied by quantitative and qualitative changes in this trade; secondly, the development within the area of new economic differentials as a result of the uneven impact of the new economy. Both of these sets of changes can be best understood if seen in the light of the economic ideas prevailing in the metropolitan countries at this time. Two of these ideas were of major importance in shaping the geography of Southeast Asia (and in converting it from an area of 'pre-developed' societies to an 'under-developed' region). At the global level there was the prevailing idea that the colonies should be developed as areas whose economy was dependent on, and complementary to, the economies of the metropolitan

[1] Leading to the partition of the old Johore–Riouw kingdom into an island sector under Dutch control and a British-controlled peninsular sector.

power. Their function was to supply raw materials, in the shape of minerals and tropical produce, which were worked up by the industries of the metropolitan country; they were also regarded as valuable markets for the expanding industries of the 'mother country'. They became increasingly specialised, with economies depending on a dangerously limited range of commodities sold in markets over which they had no control. Moreover, since any real industrial development would mean competition with the established industries of the metropolitan country, there was little attempt to build up a diversified industrial (or secondary) sector. The result was a warping of the economic structure, manifesting itself in gross inflation of the tertiary sector and a piling-up of population in the rural areas where, following the collapse of those handicraft industries which had traditionally given some degree of balance to rural life, virtually the only avenue for employment was in agriculture. And, in many parts of mainland Southeast Asia at least, this led in turn to an aggravation of the agrarian question, to the progressive decline in size of holding, to the emergence of a landless proletariat, and to the consolidation of the power of the land-owner.

The second basic theme was the emphasis on maximising the profits to be obtained from colonial development. This reinforced the tendency to specialisation in a limited range of commodities whose production gave the highest profit (not so much to the peasant as to the great commercial firms handling the trade of the region). It tended also to create an extremely patchy development pattern since the areas developed were those possessing a high degree of accessibility, those suited to the production of crops such as rubber, rice, sugar or cinchona which were needed by the metropolitan country or for which there was a ready world demand, or those possessing easily exploitable minerals. Outside these favoured areas, these 'poles of development' as we may term them, there was little development; the countryside was characterised by stagnation, if not actual retrogression, of its economic life. The general result of several decades of development under a 'liberal' or 'free-enterprise' type of economy was thus to create marked regional inequalities; these manifest themselves at the global level, in the widening gap in levels of living between the affluent nations of the 'white north' and the under-developed nations; they manifest themselves also at the local level in the contrast between the 'poles of development', such as the west coast of Malaya, or the Saigon–Cholon urban complex, and the impoverished back country. And, it is worth stressing, these regional disparities have been sharpened, if not actually created, by the processes of economic development under colonialism. This unequal development is reflected clearly in the present-day population pattern and it constitutes one of the major problems facing the new nations of Southeast Asia.

It has been suggested earlier (pp. 22–4) that the under-development of Southeast Asia was the price Southeast Asia had to pay for the development of the affluent nations of the West, that the workings of the colonial system resulted in a steady transfer of wealth from the colonial dependencies to the metropolitan country. In the succinct phrase of one expert on the under-developed world: 'While the metropole developed industry, the rest of the world developed under-development.' He adds: 'Before capitalist development there may have been *non*-developed regions; but there were no under-developed regions, much less under-developed peoples.' Capitalist development simultaneously generated development and under-development, *not* as separate processes, but *as related facets of one single process.*

The processes whereby this development = under-development equation was initiated can be seen in the history of Southeast Asia. There was the exploitation of existing societies as illustrated by the European exploitation of the Indonesian world; the spice trade, then the production of tropical raw materials under conditions of compulsory cultivation resulted in a steady draining of wealth towards northwest Europe. Where, as in Malaya, the existing societies did not offer such readily available wealth, new societies, new *semi-societies*, were created; these were concerned, as were the Chinese and Indian semi-societies created by the West in Malaya, with producing minerals and tropical raw materials needed by the metropolis—they were thus nothing more than economic appendages of the colonial power. The wealth accruing to the colonial power contributed significantly to the 'primitive accumulation of capital' on which later industrial and commercial developments in the metropolitan country were based; the developing industries of the metropolis effectively wiped out the industrial component which had been an essential element of balance in the pre-colonial society; the collapse of industry and the expanding demand for raw materials by the industries of the metropolitan country increased yet further the specialisation, the dependence, the imbalance in the colonial society.

These economic changes, which reduced a colonial area such as Southeast Asia to dependent status and thwarted any possibility of autonomous and balanced development, led also to profound dislocations in the social structure. The 'agrarianisation' of rural life resulting from the collapse of peasant handicrafts and the absence of any large-scale industrial development resulted in many areas in an increasing surplus population in the subsistence sector of the economy; the desperate plight of many country-dwellers was a powerful force driving the peasant to swell the ranks of the unemployed and under-employed in the growing cities. In contrast to conditions in the West, where the rise of capitalism shattered the old feudal structures, capitalism in its colonial form prolonged, even established, the so-called feudal or semi-feudal pattern of society as in the Annamese lands and Malaya. Most disastrous of all, the impact of capitalism created a new class—the colonial middle class; this was largely administrative and commercial in its functions and actively collaborated with the colonial power in the government and economic exploitation of the dependent territory. This was a middle class very different in its role and its character to the industrial bourgeoisie of Western Europe; in contrast to this latter, it was little interested in economic progress but was a largely parasitic group, preoccupied with grabbing such administrative crumbs as were dropped to it from the white man's table or with the high profits to be gained from trade or from money-lending. Its values and aspirations were modelled largely on those of the West and its sedulous cultivation by colonial governments served a double purpose: it alienated from the indigenous society those who should have been its natural leaders and it created a medium through which, after decolonisation, the

Plates

All photographs were taken by the author, unless otherwise stated

1. The main causeway of the great temple of Angkor Vat in Cambodia: this temple-complex represents one of the major achievements of the Hinduised civilisation of the Khmers.

2. Detail showing mediaeval Khmer life from the bas-reliefs of the Bayon (part of the Angkor complex).

SOUTHEAST ASIA—PRE-DEVELOPED

3. Tribal peoples from the uplands of North Vietnam, training as cadres at the School for National Minorities, Hanoi.

4. Khmer-leu (upland tribal people) in north-east Cambodia. These groups are typical of the less developed groups whose integration into the social and economic life of the states to which they belong poses delicate problems.

5. Khmer children in the forest zone south of Phnom Penh. Their darker skin colour and less Mongoloid features distinguish the Khmers clearly from their Vietnamese neighbours.

6. Vietnamese children, Hanoi.

7. Malay group, Kuala Lumpur. Almost one-half of the population of the region speaks languages of the Malayan group and belongs to the mixed racial type known as 'Malay'. (*By courtesy of Iain Buchanan*).

THE PEOPLES OF SOUTHEAST ASIA

8. Vietnamese Girl. Typical of the sophisticated upper group of South Vietnamese society.

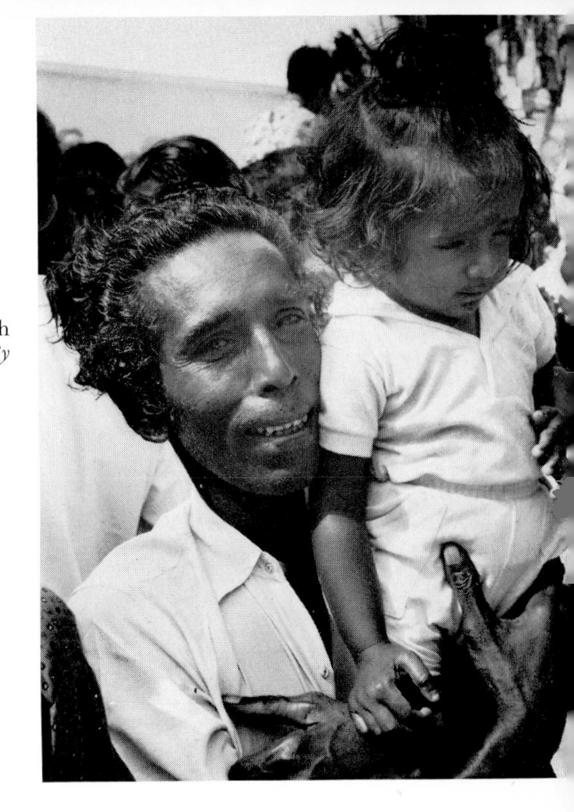

9. Father and daughter, of South Indian origin, in Singapore. (*By courtesy of Iain Buchanan*).

10. Chinese boy and young brother, Singapore. Some four-fifths of the population of this port-city are Chinese, belonging to the widely dispersed Chinese community living in the Nan-yang (i.e. the Southern Sea). These southeast Asian Chinese are largely of South Chinese origin. (*By courtesy of Iain Buchanan*)

11. Thinly settled limestone country in central Laos: bare karstic hills with forest and some cultivation at lower levels.

THE UPLANDS

12. Upland country, covered with high forest, in southern Cambodia.

THE UPLANDS

13. The rice harvest in the Red River lowland of North Vietnam. Note the tiny size of individual fields and space occupied by grave-mounds.

14. Irrigated rice-land along Malaya's west coast. A small ribbon of rice-land set in the midst of low, forested hills: seedlings just set out.

15. The lowland of east-central Cambodia during the annual summer flooding by the Mekong and its tributaries: the Mekong itself can be seen along the line of the horizon.

WET AND DRY SEASONS IN MAINLAND SOUTHEAST ASIA

16. Part of eastern Cambodia at the height of the dry season. Bare harvested ricefields, in a setting of scrub which emphasises the relatively low population pressure in this area. Settlement is linear, strung out along roads and with holdings running back into partially-cultivated woodlands. Contrast with Plate 20 which shows an area with much higher population pressure.

17. Thinly-peopled forest country in Cambodia's north-eastern province of Ratanakiri.

FOREST AND 'SAWAH'

18. Flooded ricefields (*sawahs*), with Malay home surrounded by fruit trees and flowering trees, in a forest setting. Western Malaya.

FOREST AND 'SAWAH'

19. Scattered fields of shifting cultivators on the middle slopes of the Annamite Cordillera.

CONTRASTING RURAL LANDSCAPES

20. Closely settled rice-growing countryside in southern Cambodia. Compact villages and hamlets, surrounded by trees (mainly sugar palm), and set in the midst of a chequerboard of small ricefields.

21. Hut and field of shifting cultivator in the forest zone of east-central Laos. Basic crop rice, grown as a dry crop on land temporarily cleared from forest.

CONTRASTING RURAL LANDSCAPES

22. *Chamcar* cultivation along the Mekong near Phnom-Penh. Typical of the intensive cultivation found on sandy river terrace soils in this part of Southeast Asia. Strips of land in foreground largely under vegetables and specialised crops; backland, flooded in wet season, occupied by ricefields. Settlement strung out along the crest of the *levée*.

23. Flooded ricefields in the vicinity of Malacca.

CONTRASTING RURAL LANDSCAPES

24. Contour-planting of rubber trees on rolling land in the plantation zone of western Malaya.

25. Pepper vines in the Province of Kampot, Cambodia.

GARDEN CULTIVATION

26. Intensive Chinese market gardening on moist peaty soils, Singapore island.

27. Preparing the field for transplanting rice seedlings, North Vietnam.

A VEGETABLE AND VEGETARIAN CIVILISATION
Based on the use of animal and human muscle
and on a limited range of food crops

28. Final stages of preparation of ricefield: young rice seedlings already transplanted in background, bundles of seedlings awaiting transplanting in foreground, Indian-style plough. Cambodia.

A VEGETABLE AND VEGETARIAN CIVILISATION
Based on the use of animal and human muscle
and on a limited range of food crops.

29. Small strip of cultivable land in forest country of middle Laos. A more or less passive adjustment to the potentialities of the terrain.

30. Transformation of the environment in North Vietnam. Massive deployment of peasant and military manpower to build a new series of barrages which will serve a flood-liable section of the Red River Valley. Little or no machinery; an example of the policy of 'turning labour into capital' in the shape of new development schemes which will increase the wealth (and security of life) of the peasant.

31. Village in the Red River lowland of North Vietnam, closely set within fruit trees and bamboo.

32. Small village of boat-dwelling fishing peoples on the Tonle Sap river, Cambodia.

SETTLEMENT TYPES

33. Fishing village in the south of Malaya.

SETTLEMENT TYPES

34. New middle-class housing in Singapore.

35. Side street in Hanoi, showing French architectural influence.

THE CITIES OF SOUTHEAST ASIA

36. Side street in Phnom-Penh; tree-lined boulevard showing the same French architectural influence.

37. Main street of Vientiane, Laos

38. Modern western-style bungalow housing in the suburbs of Kuala Lumpur.

39. Part of the old and congested core of Singapore's 'Chinatown'.

40. New multi-storied flats designed to rehouse part of the population of Singapore's slum areas.

41. Part of the inner harbour of Singapore, crowded with small boats engaged in the coastal or inter-island trade.

42. The problems of the Business Man: discussion outside a Singapore shop. Because of its limited resources Singapore is the trading centre *par excellence* of Southeast Asia, and its shopkeepers and traders' levels of living are vitally dependent on the free flow of trade between the various countries of Southeast Asia. It is groups such as these who felt the effects of Indonesia's 'confrontation' policy most acutely. (*By courtesy of Iain Buchanan*).

43. Films showing in Hanoi (1958): the Soviet influence is evident.

44. Cinema in Vientiane, Laos, showing Asian and Hollywood made films.

economic, social and political influences of the metropolitan country could be prolonged. Such *élite* groups today constitute one of the heaviest millstones around the necks of some of the emerging Southeast Asian peoples. . . .

Perhaps even more explosive have been the changes in the lower strata of society. The stagnation of much of the countryside, the rapid growth of population following the introduction of Western hygiene, the legacy of European education systems, with their emphasis on clerical-type learning rather than on the technical training needed to create an efficient and educated peasantry—all these have tended to bring about a swelling tide of migration from the countryside to the cities and this, in the absence of any large-scale opportunities for industrial employment, leads to an excessive inflation of the tertiary sector of the economy. Lured by the unhealthy differentials between the remuneration for pushing a pen and wielding a hoe (a differential which is another legacy of the colonial period and of European-biased educational systems) the children of the peasantry flee the stagnation of the countryside and seek the imagined opportunities of city life, only to join the ranks of the impoverished and rootless who somehow eke out a life in the crowded slums of the city.[1] Lack of structural change in agriculture, lack of any effective social or economic measures which might correct the distortions left by colonialism—these are thus intimately related to the mushroom growth of parasitic urban areas on one hand and an increasingly impoverished and backward countryside on the other. And once established, and given the type of free enterprise system bequeathed by the West to its former colonial dependencies, such differentials tend to widen by a process of 'cumulative causation'.[2] For the areas which are relatively wealthy, such as the cities, are the obvious and most desirable locations for new industrial development and this in turn adds yet further to their wealth; there is a cumulative *upward* spiral of development. And, in sharp contrast, the very stagnation of the rest of the country militates

[1] Unemployment among those in the age-group 15–19 and who are not attending school appears to be of the order of 30 per cent in Kuala Lumpur.

[2] Described by Gunnar Myrdal *op. cit.* and pre-figured by the mediaeval Arab historian Ibn Khaldun: see *An Arab Philosophy of History* (*selections from the Prolegomena of Ibn Khaldun of Tunis*), trans. C. Issawi (1950), pp. 92–3.

against that investment which might begin to wipe out stagnation and tends to encourage the exodus of the younger and more educated folk without whom real development is impossible. The result is a *downward* spiral—and a growing economic and social differential between the 'poles of development' and the back country. This is one of the major problems facing the emergent nations of Southeast Asia.

CHAPTER 7

Population: Distribution and Growth

THE TOTAL population of the Southeast Asian world is of the order of 200 million; this is larger than that of the Common Market countries and is approximately the same as that of the United States and Canada. This mass of population is extremely unevenly distributed; thus Java alone accounts for almost one-third of the region's aggregate population, crowded on to less than one-thirtieth of the region's area; by contrast, the thinly-peopled areas of Southeast Asia (density less than 50 persons per square kilometre) represent some 85 per cent of the total area. This unevenness of distribution has been accentuated by Western economic development but appears to have been a feature of the region from early times. We may adduce several factors which have contributed; some of these are environmental factors but these are strikingly reflected in the population pattern of the area through the 'prism' of man's culture.

The general nature of the area has already been described: its character as the frayed-out ends of a great mountain system margined by, or occasionally diversified by, lowland areas; of these the most striking are the great alluvial lowlands. It is these areas and their fringes, these favoured 'ecological niches', that man, first as a root-grower, then as a rice-grower, sought out and occupied from very early times. It is these areas, where life was more certain and cropping more dependable, which became the 'cradle areas' of some of the mainland peoples—the Vietnamese, the Khmers, the Thais and the Burmese; it was in these areas that, with increasingly skilful agricultural techniques, the food supply could be got to support the population which slowly accumulated over long centuries.

And, even though the density might approach figures many times that which a comparable area of European farmland might support and even though virtually empty upland country might be at hand, man made little attempt to expand his agriculture into the upland areas. This was partly because his techniques of agriculture (those of wet-rice cultivation)

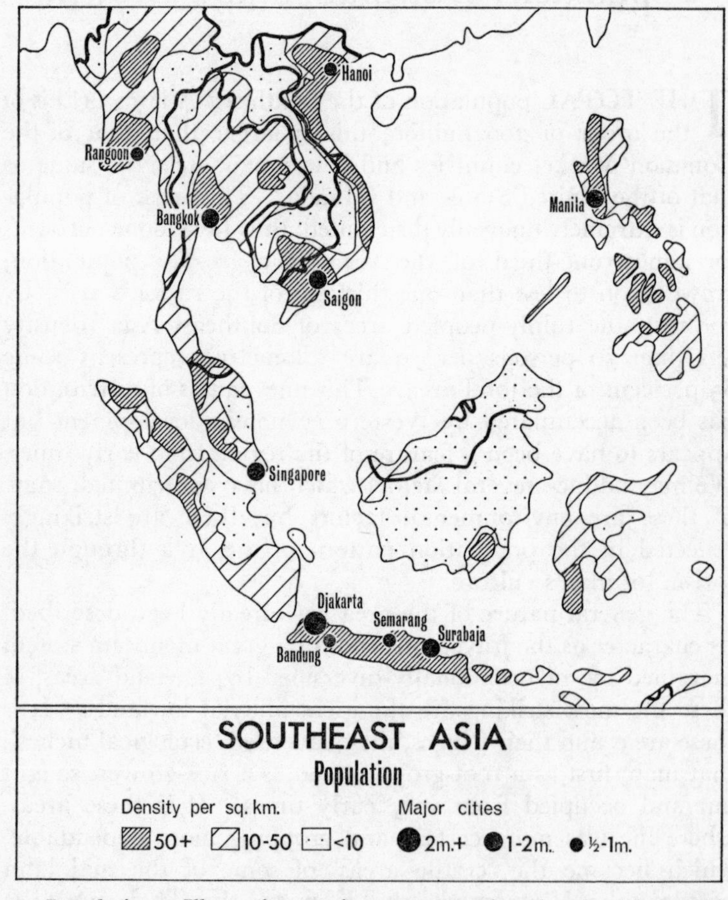

22 Population. Illustrating major concentration in the 'favourable ecological niches'—the great rice-growing areas—and the scanty population of the uplands of mainland Southeast Asia and of Borneo and part of Sumatra. Major cities (those of over half a million inhabitants) are shown.

were little suited to upland or broken terrain; partly because few Southeast Asian peoples ever developed the techniques of livestock (especially cattle) rearing which would have provided an economic basis for upland settlement; partly because much of this forested upland country was heavily malarial. The uplands therefore remained virtually empty, or were thinly occupied by weaker and backward tribal peoples practising a slash-and-burn agriculture.

Moreover, in interpreting present-day population patterns, the historical factor must be borne in mind, for some of the lowlands were occupied relatively recently in the history of the area. Perhaps the best examples are the lowlands of Lower Burma and the lowlands of Cochin China, both of which remained thinly-settled 'pioneer fringes' until the nineteenth century. In Cochin China particularly this is reflected in a much lower density of population and a larger size of land holding than in the earlier-settled coast plains of Annam or the cradle area of the Red River lowland. And in the Philippines large-scale movement from the densely populated northern islands to the relatively empty southern island of Mindanao dates largely from the present century.

Western development did not bring any great change in this general pattern. Locally, as on the basaltic 'red lands' of the Annamite cordillera, plantation development created new nuclei of population in what had been thinly-settled areas. Elsewhere, however, the upland areas were largely neglected and improved agricultural services and new varieties of food crops and commercial crops (as in Java) or improved agricultural techniques (such as the improvement of the dyke system in Tonkin) made possible an increasing accumulation of population in the already closely settled areas. It was in these latter areas, moreover, that the initial impact of improved health measures was most readily apparent; the malarial character of the uplands continued a major obstacle to the build-up of population in these areas (at least until the discovery of D.D.T.) and their scattered population, living close to survival level, provided an unfavourable environment for the dissemination of techniques of disease control. The sharp population gradient between upland and lowland persisted under these conditions, may even have increased. A further factor which influenced the population pattern and the ethnic pattern was the movement of indentured labourers towards the mines and plantations developed by the West in certain parts of Southeast Asia. The most massive of these movements was that of Chinese and Indians into the tin-mining and

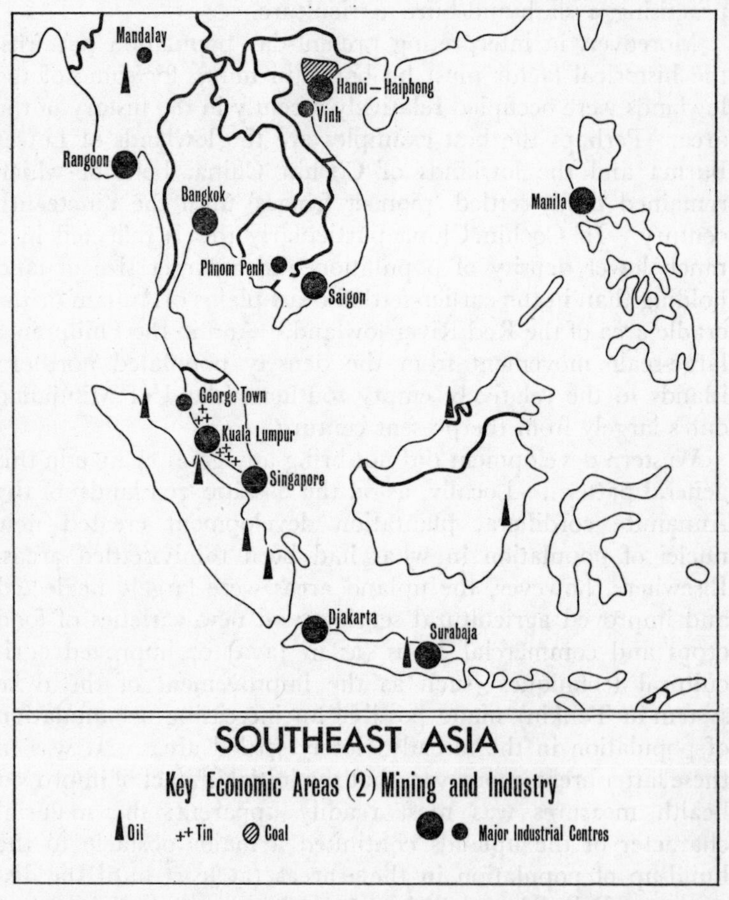

23 Key Economic Areas: Mining and Industry. Generalised distribution of major mineral deposits at present being worked is shown; no attempt is made to show *potential* areas such as the iron deposits of Laos. Industry largely concentrated in the biggest cities but in absolute and relative terms of limited importance except in North Vietnam.

rubber-growing areas of western Malaya; the scale of this was sufficient to reduce the Malay population to a minority in many areas. This creation of mixed societies, 'plural societies', or 'semi-societies', was one of the most striking results of Western economic development. The Chinese influence on Southeast Asia has already been commented on (pp. 36–7). The flow of Chinese migration, in the shape of labourers and traders, has been one of the outstanding features of the last century and today the Chinese are established in virtually every region and above all every city of the region. The greatest concentration is in the city of Singapore which has been a Chinese city from its foundation and today there are more Chinese in Southeast Asia than in Taiwan.

The major aspects of the population pattern of the area are summarised in Tables 1 and 2 below:

TABLE 1

Growth of Population in Southeast Asia, 1920–80

	1920	*1930*	*1940*	*1950*	*1960*	*1970**	*1980**
Population (millions)	108	127	150	173	219	283	364
Annual rate of increase	1·6%	1·7%	1·4%	2·4%	2·6%	2·5%	

* 'medium' variant.

By the year 2000 it is estimated that the Southeast Asian region will have an aggregate population of five hundred million. The estimated population density, in terms of the 'crude' population density and the 'nutritional' density, that is density per unit-area of cultivated land, is as shown in Table 2.

It is apparent even from this highly generalised table, that the *overall* density of population is rarely high and that in the case of some territories (Laos and the Borneo territories) the overall figure is very low indeed; it is, in fact, only slightly less than the density for New Zealand. A much more realistic picture is given by the *nutritional* density. On this basis even a thinly-peopled area such as Laos has a density per square mile of cultivated land approaching 500; in most territories it is over 750 (i.e. 290 per square kilometre) and in North Vietnam the density rivals that of some of the closely-settled parts of

TABLE 2

Crude Density and Nutritional Density, 1960

	Crude Density (per square kilometre)	*Nutritional Density*
Brunei	17	417
Burma	33	257
Cambodia	32	238
Indonesia	63	533
Laos	8	180
Federation of Malaya	53	316
Sabah	6	313
Sarawak	6	234
Singapore	2,759	11,429
Philippines	90	410
Thailand	51	262
Vietnam, North	106	1,262
Vietnam, South	83	486

China. The contrast between the two sets of indices drives home forcefully the extent to which the population is concentrated in certain favoured 'ecological niches'—the alluvial lowlands suited to rice-growing; it also draws attention to the very considerable areas of upland and savanna country which await the development of alternative types of land use, e.g. tropical livestock production, before they can be effectively integrated into the agricultural living-space of the Southeast Asian peoples.

Like many parts of the 'under-developed' world, Southeast Asia is going through a demographic revolution. Birth rates are high and death rates, though still high by Western standards, are dropping; the result is an increasing excess of births over deaths. Western Europe experienced this situation two to three generations ago but here the process of expansion was spread out over a longer period and was accompanied by a major industrial revolution; by contrast, in Southeast Asia the sudden availability of death control techniques (e.g. improved hygiene and control over malaria) has meant that the process of expansion has been much swifter—there has been a true 'population explosion'—and there has been little real economic development to support such expansion. The general picture

—and its effect on population growth—is summarised in Table 3; it will be appreciated that many of the statistics are estimates, rather than statistics with a census-based reliability.

TABLE 3

Crude Birth Rates and Death Rates, Gross Reproduction Rates and Estimated Populations in 1980

	Birth Rate	*Death Rate*	*Reproduction Rate*	*Estimated Population 1980 (thousands)*
	(per thousand)			
Brunei	49	11	—	173
Burma	43	19	2·6	35,000
Cambodia	51	20	3·3	9,810
Indonesia	52	20	2·8	152,750
Laos	—	—	—	12,693
Sabah	53	7	3·4	826
Sarawak	54	5	3·4	1,379
Singapore	38	6	2·8	3,223
Philippines	49	18	3·5	55,267
Thailand	46	13	3·2	47,516
Vietnam (North and South)	—	—	—	46,400

These figures, and especially the estimates for the 1980 population, suggest the nature of the problem facing much of the region—the problem of accommodating physically and economically, in a region where areas suited to the traditional rice economy are already heavily populated and where the economy is still largely undiversified, an increase of over 150 million people in the two decades 1960–80. Family planning, often suggested as a panacea to this problem, is in fact of only marginal relevance in confronting this immediate problem for the future workers—those who will enter the labour market in the next ten to fifteen years—are already born and so, too, are the future parents and their numbers are so large that, even if the average size of family should fall, the absolute increment of population each year will continue to be very large. Under such circumstances the only solution lies in accelerated economic development—and this may well mean labour-intensive development of the type adopted by the Chinese.

A second problem which is posed by this high rate of population growth is the very large numbers in the younger age groups; these, like the older age groups, must be supported by those in the working age group (15–59 years) with a resultant heavy burden of dependency. One of the obvious problems posed by this very large number in the school-age groups is the problem of education and this falls particularly heavily on states such as those of Southeast Asia which are striving, with limited financial and technical resources, to make 'the gigantic leap from poverty to decency'. The age structure of the population of the Southeast Asian countries is given in Table 4; figures for two developed countries are added for comparison.

TABLE 4

Age Structure of the Population

	Under 15	*15–59 years*	*60 years and over*
Brunei	46·6	47·8	5·6
Burma	41·3	53·5	5·2
Cambodia	44·7	51·3	4·0
Indonesia	42·1	53·8	4·1
Malaya	43·8	51·6	4·6
Sabah	43·5	52·6	3·9
Sarawak	44·5	50·3	5·2
Singapore	42·8	53·4	3·8
Philippines	45·7	50·0	4·3
Thailand	43·2	52·2	4·6
France	25·6	57·1	17·3
England and Wales	22·8	60·0	17·2

It will be noted that while the proportion of aged dependants is very much higher in Western Europe than in Southeast Asia, the proportion of the population aged less than 15 years is twice as high in most Southeast Asian countries. The provision of adequate schooling and technical training is even today a heavy burden in many developed countries where many decades of economic development have created the economic infrastructure on which all social services must depend. In Southeast Asia such an economic infrastructure scarcely exists. The Southeast Asian countries are in fact caught in a vicious circle in which poverty leads to inadequate schooling and poor technical training facilities and this lack in turn leads back to low productivity and poverty.

At this point one may say that the impact of the West in the shape of new techniques of death control has resulted in a major expansion of population and that, along with this

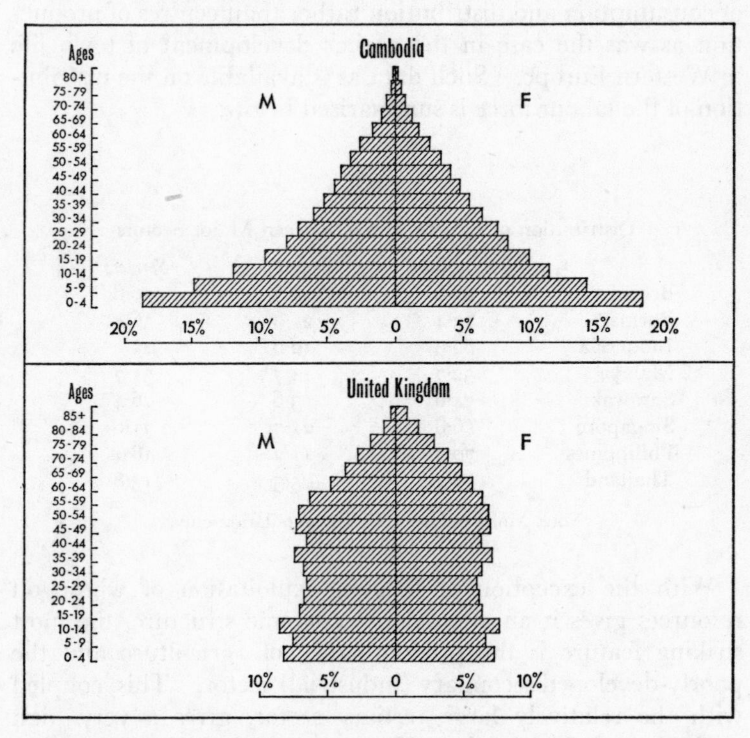

24 Contrasting Population Structures: Cambodia and the United Kingdom. Cambodia's broadly-based pyramid is typical of countries with a rapidly expanding population.

quantitative change, there has been a qualitative change of which the most obvious example is manifested in the age structure. To this one may add the changes in the occupational structure resulting less from the expansion of the secondary (i.e. industrial) sector than from the expansion of the tertiary (service) sector; this latter has been largely a result of the increase in the commercial and administrative sectors which followed westernisation and which tended to become exaggerated during the early stages of independence. These commercial-administrative middle groups are largely concentrated in the urban centres, a feature which gives many Southeast Asian cities a 'parasitic' quality—they tend to be centres of consumption and distribution rather than centres of production as was the case in the earlier development of town life in Western Europe. Such data as is available on the distribution of the labour force is summarised below:

TABLE 5

Distribution of Labour Force between Major Sectors

	Agriculture	*Industry*	*Services*
Brunei	20·6	40·7	30·6
Burma^U	12·4	21·8	56·4
Indonesia	62·9	12·0	25·1
Malaya	52·7	14·7	31·7
Sarawak	74·0	9·6	16·4
Singapore	6·8	21·7	71·0
Philippines	70·7	11·2	18·1
Thailand	78·7	5·5	13·8

Note: Males only; ^{U} = Urban population only.

With the exception of Brunei, exploitation of whose oil resources gives it an anomalous economic structure, the most striking feature is the predominance of agriculture and the poorly-developed secondary (industrial) sector. This, coupled with the relatively large tertiary sector, gives a very high tertiary:secondary ratio; this is approximately twice that typical of developed Western countries and it is a sector that is largely urban-concentrated.

One of the distinctive features of the most recent period has been the rapid growth of the urban sector. Southeast Asia has a long tradition of urban life but many of the bigger and most rapidly-growing centres are, in terms of the history of the area, of relatively recent origin; an example is Singapore. The degree of urbanisation varies; in Malaya about two-fifths of the population is urban, in the Philippines somewhat less than one-third, while in countries such as Cambodia or Thailand it is much smaller—between one-eighth and one-tenth of the population is classed as urban; this may be compared with proportions of almost three-fifths in France and over four-fifths in England and Wales. The proportion living in cities of over 100,000 is more uniform; for most Southeast Asian countries it appears to be of the order of one-tenth. The pace of urbanisation has accelerated greatly in recent years and, in the case of the larger centres, the rate of growth is considerably in excess of the rate of growth of the population of the country concerned; thus Kuala Lumpur between 1947 and 1957 was growing at the rate of 6·2 per cent per annum, as against a national average of 2·9 per cent; Djakarta was growing (1955–59) at a rate of 10·8 per cent annually as compared with the Indonesian national average of 2·0 per cent; Bangkok (1947–60) at a rate twice the average for Thailand as a whole. Such growth rates reflect a steady stream of migration from the rural areas and they give rise to a multitude of urban problems: housing and transportation difficulties, shortage of essential services such as water and sewerage, spiralling land prices and many social maladjustments. The relative wealth of the cities attracts consumer-oriented industries and a disproportionate share of the country's professionally-trained personnel (in Thailand there is one doctor to 3,000 inhabitants in the urban areas as against one to 30,000 inhabitants in the countryside) and the result, as pointed out in Chapter 9, is a widening gap between a stagnating or slowly developing countryside and the ostentatious and precariously-based wealth of a handful of urban areas. This growing divergence between the rural and urban sectors of society is found in most of the so-called 'underdeveloped' countries and is an important factor making for instability; only by careful national planning and real rural development can the roots of the problem be attacked. And, as the American economist Robert Heilbroner has observed, in an environment such as Southeast Asia, such economic development 'is *not primarily an economic but a political and social process*'.[1] It is the process of creating, by far-reaching political and social changes, the type of society within which wealth

[1] Robert Heilbroner, *The Great Ascent* (New York, 1963), p. 24.

can be created and in which employment, incomes and levels of living can be progressively raised. Such attempts to create the pre-conditions for economic development which will sustain their rapidly growing populations form an important theme in the recent history of the states of Southeast Asia.

CHAPTER 8

The Emergence of the New State Pattern

EUROPEAN CONTROL in Southeast Asia never completely extinguished the forces of nationalism; these remained a strong, if hidden, undercurrent in the life of the region, manifesting themselves in many forms. Sometimes the form was a literary form, as in the writings of Rizal in the Philippines; sometimes they showed themselves in industrial unrest and labour disputes as in Indochina; sometimes they focused on some aspect of traditional life: the Throne in Cambodia, the Buddhist faith in Burma and parts of Vietnam or Islam in parts of the Indies. But in whatever form it manifested itself nationalism remained muted; it seemed incapable of challenging the power of the great colonial empires between which most of Southeast Asia was divided. Only Thailand, by the astuteness of its leaders, succeeded in retaining a precarious political independence; the rest of this vast area was partitioned between the British, the Dutch, the French and the Americans (with part of the island of Timor remaining as a reminder of the former imperial greatness of Portugal).

The Second World War changed this situation. The rapid advance of the Japanese destroyed the myth of European invincibility while in the Japanese-controlled areas nationalist feeling took on a new lease of life, either as a result of encouragement by the Japanese or in reaction against the Japanese-supported administrations. These forces, combined with a changed world attitude to colonialism in general, made the whole colonial structure in Southeast Asia increasingly unstable. In the Philippines legislation as far back as 1934 provided for full independence, to be achieved over a period of ten years; this independence was proclaimed in 1946. More far-reaching in its impact, however, was the achievement of independence by India in 1947. This was followed by the

25 The Political Pattern of Southeast Asia, 1966. Only Portugal succeeds in retaining a colony of the old type.

granting of independence to Burma (effective from early 1948) and the achievement of independence by Indonesia in 1949. The states of French Indochina (Cambodia, Laos and Vietnam) achieved their independence after a protracted and bitter colonial war in 1954, though at the price of a temporarily-divided Vietnam. Malaya, after a long state of insurgency and after more localised guerrilla warfare, became independent in 1957.

The relatively simple pattern of colonial days was replaced by a more complex pattern of almost a dozen separate national entities. These differ greatly in population—from Laos whose population may be between two and five millions to Indonesia which, with a population of close on 100 million, is the fourth largest nation on earth. They differ greatly in their resource endowment and, a legacy of the colonial period, in their economic orientation. Above all, they differ widely in their external alignments and the nature of their political systems. Some, like Thailand, the Philippines or South Vietnam, are Western-oriented, are parts of a Western defence system designed to contain a hypothetical Chinese expansion; North Vietnam is part of the socialist or communist camp; Burma, Indonesia and above all Cambodia have succeeded in remaining neutral in the face of considerable external pressures; Laos lacks any effective unity and is deeply split by Cold War rivalries. And the range of political systems adopted by these countries includes the thinly-veiled authoritarianism of South Vietnam or Thailand, the Buddhist socialism of Burma or Cambodia (the former a republic, the latter a monarchy), the 'guided socialism' of Indonesia, the communism of North Vietnam, the attempt at an American-style democracy in the Philippines, and the organised confusion of Laos where the struggle between the West and the communist bloc has been superimposed on older, regionally-based, clan rivalries.

Yet beneath this patchwork of diversities these Southeast Asian states face many common problems and in this, and the confrontation of these problems, we can detect certain themes which run through the political and economic emergence of this half a score states. One might perhaps go further and say that these themes are common not merely to the countries of Southeast Asia but to all the countries of the under-developed world. They all face a poverty (emphasised by food intake levels or *per capita* incomes) which is partly the result of the difficulties posed by a tropical environment, partly the result of the colonially-retarded and undiversified character of their economies. This poverty is aggravated by the rapid expansion of their populations and it is thrown into sharp emphasis by the growing divergence between their living levels and the rising living levels of the affluent nations. It is, moreover, a poverty which is becoming increasingly intolerable as an awareness of their poverty spreads among even the most remote and disinherited peoples. A century ago, even twenty-five years ago, such an awareness scarcely existed; one of the major results of improved communications (of the 'shrinking of the globe') has been to create an awareness that poverty is not inevitable, not something pre-ordained, that the hunger of one's children, their limited chances of survival, and the absence for them of the schooling and the economic development which would ensure for them a meaningful future—all these things are within man's power to correct. It is this growing belief that man has it in his power to shape the future which provides the motive force behind what has been termed 'the revolution of rising expectations'. These attitudes involve the Southeast Asian peoples at the personal, individual level; there is also an important shift in attitudes at the national level. These countries have for long been the *objects* of world diplomacy and this is a role they are rejecting increasingly, aspiring instead (and the United Nations offers an opportunity for this) to play the role of *active subjects* on the international scene.

This trend is part of what Richard Harris has termed 'the revolution of equality', and in an area such as Southeast Asia this shows itself in several forms. First, there is the drive for total independence, involving a rejection of Western dominance of any sort, the rejection of alliances which may seem to threaten the emergent nations' freedom of action, and a trend towards neutrality and nonalignment (e.g. Cambodia, Burma). This may have internal repercussions, involving the rejection of governments which are regarded as insufficiently independent and of bases and treaty ties which seem to encroach upon the ideal of total independence. Secondly, there is what may be termed, for want of a better term, 'the cultural revolution'. This is in part a reaction against the tendency of the former colonial régimes to relegate the traditional or indigenous culture to second place. In part it is what we shall later term 'the search for roots'—the reassertion of those cultural elements —language, religion, institutions or dress—which had been pushed into the background by the more aggressive culture of the West. As manifested today in Southeast Asia it shows itself in the rejection of the more tawdry and commercialised aspects of Western culture (the 'yellow culture' decried by some Singapore politicians), the emphasis on local languages rather than on European languages (e.g. the emphasis on Malay in Malaysia), the integration into modern political life of earlier political forms (e.g. the traditions of the Khmer empire in contemporary Cambodia), and the strong assertion of the value of the traditional religious systems (e.g. Buddhism in Burma, Cambodia and Vietnam). Thirdly, there is 'the administrative revolution'—the drive to wipe out corruption and to create an efficient administration capable of running the country in such a way that national pride is satisfied and the visiting foreigner will come away with the impression that the country is in no way inferior to any others; such a drive may, in its initial stages, involve a shift towards authoritarian forms of government.

Southeast Asia today shows many manifestations of this 'revolution of equality' and, indeed, it is a process through which most newly-independent countries go. Some of the manifestations—such as the trend towards a total neutralism, based on a strong nationalism which rejects fiercely any external attempts at interference, we find difficult to understand, tending (a legacy of the early 1950s) to equate neutrality with communism or at least pro-communist tendencies. Yet trends towards such a revolution can be discerned over the whole of Southeast Asia, with the exception of countries such as Thailand which are politically backward or countries like South Vietnam whose régimes depend on American support —and even in these countries it is inevitable sooner or later. And sooner or later, too, this 'revolution of equality' will be followed by a revolution in society, designed to achieve those structural changes in the social system, such as agrarian reform, which are imperative if poverty is to be eliminated and modern and diversified economies, which alone will ensure for the individual a secure and meaningful future, are to be created.

We can best understand the political geography of Southeast Asia if we discard the static and descriptive approach and instead regard the area as an area whose peoples are trying to break the shackles of poverty and create the new political forms which alone can make possible, as we shall see in Chapter 10, real and self-sustaining economic development and, with this development, genuine political independence. Some of the problems the area faces have already been briefly alluded to (they are problems common to many countries of the 'underdeveloped' world) and these, and the fashions in which Southeast Asia's peoples are confronting them, may be commented on more fully.

We must first draw attention to a fundamental contrast with the European societies with which we are more familiar. In this Euro-American world (and including the U.S.S.R. in this context) economic development took place within existing societies which had been created over a relatively long period of time. In the Southeast Asian world—and the underdeveloped world as a whole—such national societies scarcely exist (cp. pp. 76–7 on the ethnic fragmentation of Southeast Asia) and a prime essential is 'the creation, forcibly or otherwise, of workable institutional structures'. This includes not merely a strong and coherent state, whose principles of organisation may differ in many respects from the Western forms with which we are familiar but also an effective mobilisation (encadrement) of the masses. In the absence of this, the technical and cultural vacuum noted by Danilo Dolci in even an area such as southern Europe becomes an abyss in an area as impoverished and exploited as Southeast Asia, an abyss separating the masses and the pitifully small *élite* groups and which effectively blocks any real development drive.

One of the most important aspects of the political geography of Southeast Asia is the search for national identity. These countries have emerged from colonial status with no well-defined, clearly-marked national territories. Their boundaries were little more than a legacy of the adjustments and accommodations made by the representatives of the colonial powers; they were, moreover, boundaries which showed little regard for the ethnic or historical realities of the area. Today, in Southeast Asia, we are witnessing a desperate drive on the part of the emergent nations to assert their national individuality. This process shows itself at two levels. Superficially, it shows itself in the proliferation of national flags and emblems, and of national languages and by the multiplication of embassies, legations and all the external trappings of a modern state. At a deeper level it shows itself in the turning-back to the vanished glories of an earlier period. History, myth and legend become important forces in the creation of a national consciousness; the legendary *garuda* or the ruins of Angkor reappear as national emblems, as integrating factors in the new states of Southeast Asia. And, as Jean Chesneaux observes: 'This presence of a distant past is all the more vigorous since, in the majority of cases, the Afro-Asian countries, today under-developed, have been pre-developed countries whose civilised traditions are older than those of Germany or Gaul'. This 'cult of the past' is an important theme in many Southeast Asian countries; the glories of the medieval Khmer Empire provide an inspiration and a model for contemporary Cambodia, just as the resistance of the great historic figures of Vietnam to outside aggression inspires many who fight in Vietnam today. At the same time, as other French observers have commented, it is not without its perils for 'those who can survive only by a furious drive towards the future'.

The concentration of political power, whether in the hands of a strong ruler or a dominant or single political party, is a second theme. This stems from the social conditions of the countries of Southeast Asia and, above all, from the absence of any *effective* middle group between the masses and the ruler or the ruling group; this, in turn, is a result of the economic and educational backwardness which was one of the legacies of colonialism. Given such conditions, many of the nations organise themselves around a charismatic ruler—a Sihanouk, a Sukarno or a Ho Chi Minh—who incarnates the successful struggle for independence. This concentration of political power, arising from the over-riding need for stability and from the inadequate encadrement of the new states, shows itself also in the dominant—or single-party governments of Southeast Asia. The immediate post-independence experience of these new nations (as in Cambodia) showed that multi-party systems of government (on classic Western-democratic lines) led to an expensive and sometimes destructive dispersion of social and political energies. On the other hand, the obliteration of all diversity, of all opposition, may mean a monolithic sterility. The system of a dominant party (or a system such as Cambodia's Popular Socialist Community) represents an attempt at compromise between these two extremes. Such a dominant party serves as the pivot of the country's political life and the opportunity it provides for the system's less powerful groups to express their opinion offsets to some degree the dangers of sterility (this is the pattern of the Asian communist régimes; variants upon it are the Malaysian and Indonesian patterns).

A third important theme in Southeast Asia is the striving to bridge the great gap between the masses and the small *élite* groups, to integrate the common man more effectively into the political life of the country. Where the country is small and relatively homogeneous linguistically this can be done by the direct contact of the Head of State with the masses. Radio, television, the plane—all these technological developments help to bridge the gap between the leader and the people. Today, indeed, the radio and the helicopter are playing in some Southeast Asian countries the same unifying role as did the Roman road system in Western Europe two millennia ago. Such developments, however, are little more than temporary expedients and they do not represent any real solution to the problem in countries with populations as large as that of Indonesia or where the population, though small, is fragmented either by geographic isolation or by linguistic barriers (e.g. Laos, upland Vietnam or the Shan States of Burma). Under these conditions, social, economic and political development depends on the encadrement, the mobilisation of the masses. It was Stalin who claimed that, of all the forms of capital, the most precious and decisive was represented by a country's cadres and, whatever else of Stalin's concepts may have been discarded, this remains the golden rule—or the iron rule—of real and self-sustaining development in a backward country.

In Southeast Asia the basis for such an encadrement is provided by the dominant political party or ideology organised around a charismatic leader: the Lao Dong party and Ho Chi Minh in North Vietnam, the Popular Socialist Community and Prince Norodom Sihanouk in Cambodia, the People's Action Party and Lee Kuan-yew in Singapore or the ideology of Marhaenism which has grown out of Sukarno's thinking. In these states the possibility of creating the political preconditions for economic progress exists; it is in some cases a tenuous possibility since it depends still largely on the ability of one man—the leader—but even this tenuous prospect has not yet taken shape in a racially-divided Malaysia, a Laos or South Vietnam where external interference precludes any real development or a Philippines which is struggling, in the midst of corruption, an explosive agrarian situation, and personal ambitions, to make a Western form of democracy work. And if we look outwards to the rest of the Third World the faltering pace of social and economic development in the majority of newly-emergent states is largely a reflection of the failure to create, through encadrement, any adequate infrastructure for such development.

Finally, the political geography—and through it the social geography—of the countries has been shaped by two sets of forces. The first is the influence of colonialism, of the continuing economic dominance of the West which is labelled 'neo-colonialism', and of the Cold War rivalries of the last two decades; this set of forces is commented on in Chapter 10. Secondly, and this is inevitable given the political structures we have described, the role of gifted or dedicated individuals who have guided their nations through the stormy period since independence. The geography of South Vietnam was shaped as profoundly by the 'personalism' of Ngo Dinh Diem as that of North Vietnam is by the communism of Ho Chi Minh; to understand contemporary Cambodia without some reference to the concepts of 'royal socialism' as propounded by Prince Norodom Sihanouk is as impossible as the attempt to understand Indonesia without reference to the ideas of Sukarno. In Southeast Asia, as indeed in many parts of the 'under-developed' world, the geographer has to concern himself not merely with the political ideologies which are shaping the new nation-states but also, and increasingly, with the personalities of the charismatic leaders who enshrine and interpret these ideologies.

CHAPTER 9

The Nations of Southeast Asia

BEFORE WE proceed to sketch in the broad lineaments of the contemporary social geography of the nations of Southeast Asia it is as well to recall some of the outstanding features of the area: a population of over 200 million, growing as rapidly as the population of any region on earth and showing a very great human diversity. A region of 'moonlight civilisations', reflecting the luminous quality of the great civilisations of Hindu India, China and, more distantly, Islam, whose development was interrupted by the impact of colonialism, whose peoples were sometimes arbitrarily divided by the new boundaries imposed by the colonial powers and whose economies were warped (or retarded) by colonialism. A tropical region yet with a great variety of environmental conditions, possessing a diversity of resources and enjoying the unusual advantage of a high degree of accessibility by water. A region in which perhaps the most striking common features are poverty (measured in terms of the usual indices such as *per capita* income or calorie intake) and which, caught up like the rest of the ex-colonial world in the 'revolution of rising expectations', is showing an increasing determination to wipe out this poverty, whose peoples are increasingly unwilling to accept the status of second-grade citizens in our global society or the status for their countries of second-grade states, mere pawns in the policies of the great powers.

The processes of political and social change, whereby Southeast Asia's peoples are seeking to remould the older order (and in this process of remoulding are transforming the region's geography) show a great diversity and in this chapter an

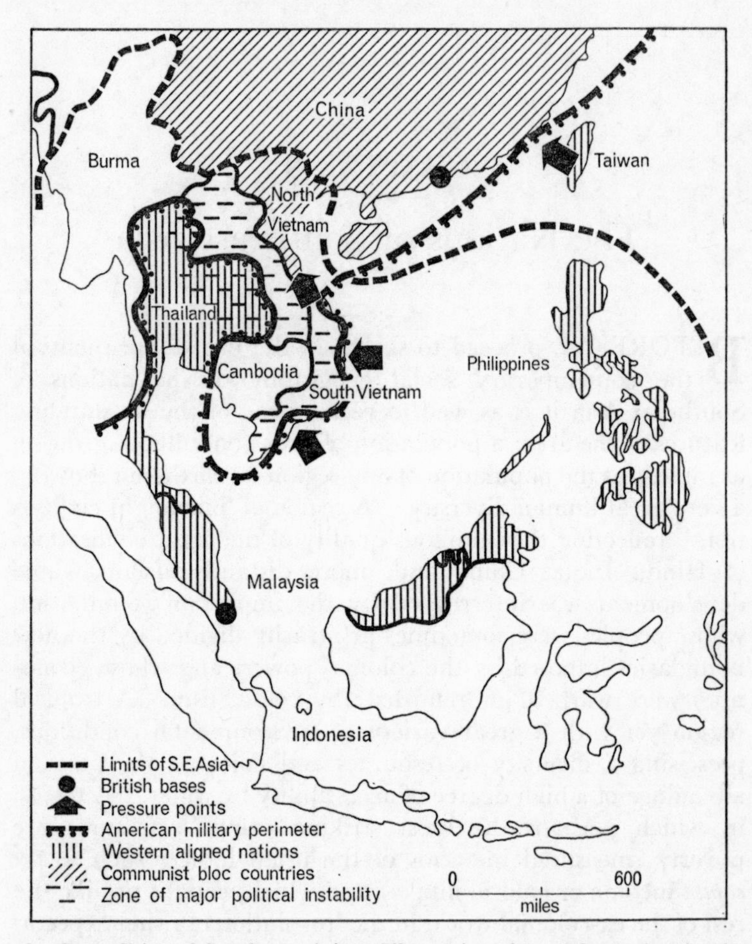

26 Geopolitics of Southeast Asia. Illustrating the confrontation in the area of the two major power blocs—those of the United States and of the Communist World. The extension of America's military perimeter from her Pacific island bases on to the Southeast Asia mainland in South Vietnam and Thailand involves her directly in the internal conflicts of Southeast Asia; the zone of contact between the capitalist and communist worlds is a zone of civil war and of 'national liberation struggles', stretching from Laos to the southern tip of Vietnam.

attempt will be made to convey to the reader something of this diversity.

We may group these dozen or so nations in various ways. We may, for example, group them on the basis of their cultural heritage into those strongly influenced by the Chinese cultural tradition (Vietnam), those influenced by Hindu India (Cambodia, Thailand, Burma and, in part, Laos), those influenced by Islam (Malaysia and Indonesia) and those moulded by Spanish Catholicism (the Philippines). We may group them on the basis of their past colonial experience—French, British, Dutch, American; this experience has left a more obvious, though perhaps more superficial and less enduring legacy than that of China, India or Islam. We may also group these countries in terms of their relationship to the two great power-blocs—the Western or capitalist world and the socialist world; on this basis we would distinguish pro-Western countries (essentially the SEATO countries of Thailand, the Philippines and South Vietnam but including also Malaysia); the communist-bloc countries (North Vietnam); and the nonaligned nations (Burma, Cambodia, Indonesia and increasingly Singapore). This latter grouping is perhaps the most significant since a country's external alignment, in Southeast Asia at least, is usually a reflection of its internal political structure and this in turn strongly influences the character of its social and economic geography. Thus, the nonaligned nations are generally moving towards a socialist type of economy, though this 'socialism' is very different from the 'classic' Western socialism and contains a strong national component (e.g. Cambodian socialism, or the Marhaenism of Indonesia). North Vietnam is part of the communist bloc and its economy, in both its agrarian and its industrial sector, follows the communist pattern of development as illustrated by China. The Western-bloc countries are characterised by a largely free-enterprise type of economy with little effective economic planning and economies heavily shored-up by external aid and loans. As for Laos, the country can be scarcely said to have an 'economy' in any meaningful sense. The major features of the countries in each of these groups are examined in more detail below.

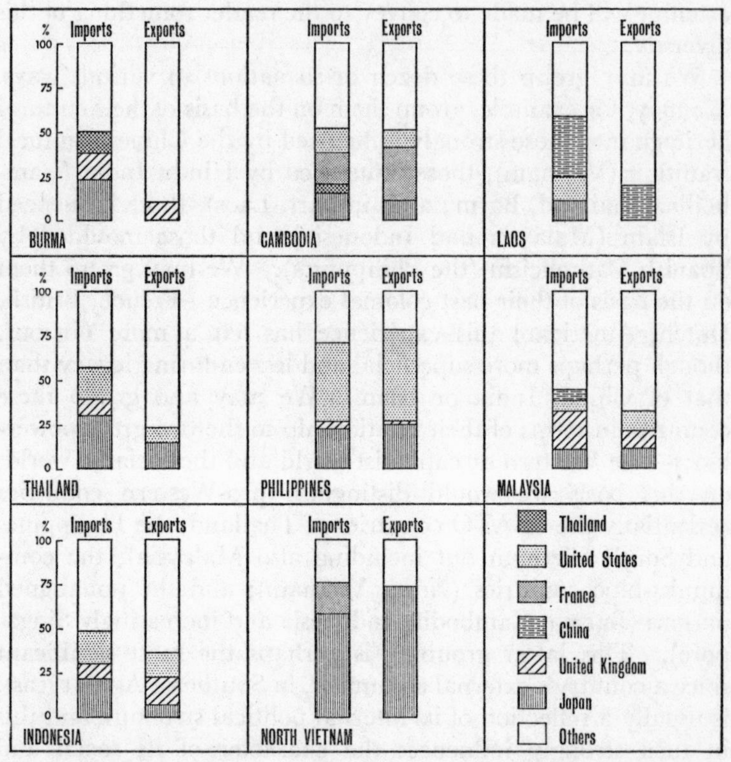

27 The Trading Relations of the Southeast Asian Nations. Note dominant role of the U.S.A. in Filipino commerce and the significance of Japan, especially as a source of imports (North Vietnamese figures *exclude* trade with the communist bloc).

(A) The Non-aligned Countries of Southeast Asia

The concept of nonalignment, of positive neutrality, among the emergent nations of the Third World has been, in part at least, a reaction against the ill-considered haste and thinly-disguised pressures with which the two protagonists in the Cold War—the U.S.A. and the U.S.S.R.—sought to extend their following of client-states. The concept is tied in with the idea of a Third Force, a group committed to neither the Western nor the communist camp,[1] and it emerged clearly at the

[1] It seems implicit in the views of these two major blocs that such a third bloc can be only transient; such a view may, however, underestimate the strength of a nationalism which may prove as resistant to communism as to capitalism.

Bandung Conference in 1955. The great bloc
colonial territories, controlling a sizeable propo
votes in the United Nations, might *potentially* play a
in the councils of the world organisation, but onl
they acted with a strong sense of solidarity. For a
reasons such unified action never emerged, but the
forward at Bandung have provided the corner-ston of their foreign policy for a number of nations, notably India under Nehru, Sukarno's Indonesia and the Buddhist socialisms of Burma and Cambodia. In the case of the two latter states their small size and their vulnerability are strong factors predisposing their rulers to a neutralist path; the unedifying example of their neighbours (i.e. Laos and South Vietnam) who have allowed themselves to become involved in the cold war antagonisms of the great powers drives home the lesson that in neutralism alone can be found the peace essential if the problems of economic development are to be solved.

(*I*) *CAMBODIA*

Cambodia offers the most striking and successful example of nonalignment in Southeast Asia; its development during the last decade also illustrates the role which can be played by the charismatic ruler.

The country is small and was until a little over a decade or so ago a French protectorate. Its resources were not such as to attract any major economic development, and it thus escaped the sociological problems a richer area might have inherited. For centuries it has been strongly Buddhist and, even under colonial rule, the Khmer monarchy retained the reverence of the masses and provided a historical continuity which links the present Head of State, Prince Norodom Sihanouk, with the kings of the medieval empire of Angkor. These elements were to prove of major importance in the evolution of Cambodia's 'royal socialism'.

When the country became fully independent Cambodia, like many other newly-emergent nations, experimented with Western-style parliamentary democracy. The experiment was a failure, for the sterile struggle of what claimed to be parliamentary parties absorbed most of the energies needed to bring about modernisation and economic development. Under these circumstances Prince Norodom Sihanouk, then King, abdicated in order to be better able to devote himself to politics and it was from his ideas that the Popular Socialist Community was derived. This is essentially an experiment in direct democracy and it has succeeded in integrating various traditional elements—the socialist content of Buddhism, the strong tradition of rural co-operation and the loyalty to the throne—into a new political form. It is socialist, yet rejects both Marxism, which leaves small place for nationalism, and the class struggle, aiming instead at 'a less sharp and less unjust separation of classes'.[1]

The country's economy is a planned economy, aiming at a modest but realistic increase in *per capita* levels of living, aiming at a wider dispersion of industry and a reduction of the differences in quality of life and of opportunities between country and town. This latter expresses itself in a social and educational drive which is facilitated by the traditions of rural co-operation and mutual aid referred to above and by the fact that the Buddhist priesthood has kept alive the tradition of rural education, even if such education were largely religious. And Cambodians see a prototype of this policy of emphasising the well-being of the common man in the earlier history of their country, above all in the policies of the mediaeval Khmer emperor Jayavarman VII. The economy is a 'mixed' economy, that is, one in which private enterprise, state enterprise and mixed enterprise (part state, part private) all play a role. But the mainspring of Cambodia's policy of modernisation is the industrial sector and in this sector the largest units are state-controlled, consisting of factories donated by the Chinese People's Republic. This dominance of the state was inevitable, given the absence of any sizeable national bourgeoisie possessing either the means of production or the capital to acquire such means. And the state control over the economy has been extended by the state take-over of the banking and the import-export sectors in 1964; only thus can the conditions for effective economic planning be created.

[1] A policy favoured, incidentally, by the absence of sharply conflicting class groups, an absence due in turn to the relative lack of economic development under the colonial régime.

The individuality of Cambodia shows itself very clearly in its external politics. Alone among the countries of Indochina it has managed to preserve an effective neutrality. It is a neutrality which forms one of the corner-stones of the whole Cambodian experiment and if indeed it is in part imposed by the logic of Cambodia's geopolitical position (in the dangerous 'shatter belt' where the Western and communist blocs confront one another) it has none the less had to be fought for and, once gained, carefully guarded. The fate of Laos or of South Vietnam illustrates the dangers of involvement; it is one of Sihanouk's greatest achievements that he not only recognised the dangers but has been able by his diplomatic finesse to avert them from his country. The Cambodian attitude on these matters is clear: they want neither the American nor the Russian nor the Chinese way of life. 'Quite simply we want to follow the Cambodian way of life.' Such an attitude has involved an avoidment of military pacts, the rejection of conditional aid, and an increasing tendency on the part of the country to turn down all outside aid and to rely for its development solely on its own resources and its people's efforts.

(II) THE UNION OF BURMA

The wide diversity of politico-geographic conditions within the Southeast Asian world is emphasised by the contrast between the Kingdom of Cambodia and the Union of Burma. Both, it is true, were formerly colonial dependencies; both are dominantly Buddhist by religion and both are 'socialist' in terms of their internal politics and 'nonaligned' in external politics. But there the similarities end; in almost every other respect, including their degrees of success in confronting the problem of under-development, the contrasts between the two countries are both sharp and far-reaching.

Burma[1] has been described as 'a creation of the armed diplomacy and administrative convenience of late nineteenth-century Imperialism'; in contrast to Cambodia, which has long preserved a high degree of territorial cohesion, the pre-European period in Burma was characterised by a series of

[1] In the account which follows I have drawn heavily on Leach's study, *The Political future of Burma* (see Bibliography, p. 168).

indigenous but territorially unstable régimes. The territory bounded by the artificial borders inherited from the British colonial period consists of half a dozen more or less distinct territorial and human entities; these may be listed as follows:

1. *The Burmese cradle area, or 'heartland'.* This cradle area, as commented earlier (p. 42), consists, like the other cradle areas of Southeast Asia, of an alluvial lowland, a moist aquatic environment, suited to a rice-based civilisation. In the northern section it takes in part of the Dry Zone of central Burma and here close settlement and a highly developed civilisation were dependent on massive irrigation works; this was the centre of the old Burmese kingdom focusing on Ava and later on Mandalay. The southern sector, with a wetter monsoonal climate, was effectively integrated into the Burmese core area during the period of British control in the early nineteenth century. Previous to the colonial period it was, like the delta of the Mekong, thinly-occupied but today is the major zone in terms of both population and rice production. Within this 'Burmese heartland' most of the population are Burmese-speaking and Buddhist by religion.

2. *The Arakan coastal strip.* The population of this zone is Burmese-speaking but the region has tended to have a separate and distinctive political history. It is isolated by the physical barriers of mountain and river from the heartland and has significant cultural links with the Chittagong area and East Pakistan, e.g. it has a sizeable Moslem minority.

3. *The Shan states and Karenni.* This is a region whose inhabitants speak languages different from Burmese and who fall into two groups—the dominant Shan minority and the hill people known collectively as Palaung. In the past it was a patchwork of tiny principalities; today, in theory at least, the Shan State and the Kayah State are components of the federal Union of Burma and, as such, enjoy a considerable measure of autonomy. Culturally, no major divide separates the Shans of Burma from the Shans of southwest China, Laos or Thailand and they have never been effectively integrated into the

Burmese state. Leach foresees the future of this zone as that of a buffer zone 'where sovereignty remains unprecise but Chinese political influence predominates'.

4. *The Kachin State.* This takes in much of the wetter and heavily-forested mountain country of the extreme north. It is an area where past missionary activity created a small *élite* group of Western-educated Christians; these tend to look down on their Burmese Buddhist counterparts whose level of education and training is lower. The Kachin state has none the less shown a strong loyalty towards the central government; the heavy subsidisation of the state from central government funds reflects the government's awareness of this and of the extreme importance of Kachin loyalty. Yet the Kachin area has never been assimilated effectively into the Burmese state, even during the colonial period, and the pressures for greater autonomy suggest that the government of an independent Burma has been no more successful in this respect than its colonial predecessor.

5. *The Western frontier zone.* Shows similar characteristics to the Kachin area though the dominant groups are Nagas or Chins. Much of the north of this zone has long been controlled by the White Flag communists; these are perhaps best classed as 'Mao-ist' or 'pro-Chinese' in ideological terms.

6. *The Karen zone of the south.* Here the majority of the population are Buddhists with a rice economy and culture very similar to that of Burma proper. Ever since Burma became independent the Karens have been in more or less continuous armed conflict with the central government. This Karen separatism derives its impetus from two sources—the traditional hostility of the local 'Talaings' (or Mons) to the Burmese of the Dry Zone and the hostility of the Christianised *élite* groups among the upland Karens to the dominantly Buddhist central government.

The tensions within the Union of Burma are thus a legacy

of a European colonial policy which showed little concern for ethnic and cultural realities when the frontiers of the former colonies were demarcated; the inevitable difficulties resulting from this lack of awareness have been aggravated by the uneven impact of the West (above all the impact of missionary activity) and by a colonial policy based on the concept of 'divide and rule' which did little to break down the suspicion and distrust with which many minority peoples regarded the Burmese. Today, and this is in marked contrast to, say, Cambodia, it can be claimed, with some justification, that 'the unity of Burma is a map-maker's fiction' (E. R. Leach). The latest data on ethnic composition is provided by the 1931 Census; according to this, some two-thirds of the population was Burmese (a proportion possibly exaggerated) while the remaining one-third was made up, in approximately equal proportions, by four groups—the Shans, the Karens, the Arakanese, and 'others'. However, since the density in the Burmese heartland is relatively high (between 150 and 230 per square mile) and that in some of the tribal areas as low as 10–30 per square mile, the proportion of the total area of the country occupied by non-Burmese is much higher than their absolute numbers might suggest. As is the case in other parts of Southeast Asia, some of the group names (e.g. Karen, Kachin) are derogatory, implying 'slave-barbarian'; they are, moreover, often 'bulk categories' encompassing a great variety of tribal sub-groups. Only the Karens and the Talaings are not parts of larger ethnic groupings overlapping into adjoining countries and in all cases the prospects of effective assimilation to the dominant Burmese group are negligible. These groups form part of a great patchwork of tribal peoples extending from the Naga Hills of Assam to the uplands of Vietnam who occupy the 'twilight zone' between the high civilisations of South and Southeast Asia (Figure 12). And in Burma at least the shape of their future, above all their relationships to the country of which they are nominally citizens, is still uncertain.

As far as the indigenous socio-political system was concerned the colonial period was negative and far-reaching in its impact. The existing Burmese systems of government, reaching down to the village level, were completely erased and replaced by a bureaucracy modelled on that developed by the British in India (of which country, indeed, Burma was regarded as part). The whole system rested ultimately on military coercion relying on the use of Indian troops in the non-Burmese tribal areas and of troops drawn from the hill peoples to maintain order in Burma proper. The Burmese government to which power passed in 1948 was thus confronted by the need to rebuild society from the village level upwards and at the same time to overcome the aggravated group antagonisms inherited from this British policy of 'divide and rule'. By and large it has chosen the path of least resistance and retained an administrative pattern similar to that of pre-Independence days; it has, moreover, continued the colonial policy of using one group against another whenever coercion was necessary.

The pattern of political development has been complex; the dominant theme has been the attempt to evolve a Burmese socialist state. As in Cambodia, the initial experiment with Western political models proved fruitless and there has been a gradual reassertion of traditional and indigenous (i.e. Buddhist) elements. In the immediate post-independence period there was a strong drive on the part of Burma's *élite* group (dominantly Marxist at that time) to create a Burmese socialist state, 'Marxist in form and nationalist in content'. The group was never strong enough, nor possessed of a sufficiently broad popular base, to achieve this and during the U Nu administration (U Nu can be regarded as one of the great charismatic leaders who emerged in Southeast Asia after the Second World War) there was a strong trend away from Marxism to a Buddhist socialism, pragmatic in its character but representing, in its essence, a return to the traditional values of the Burmese people.[1] This 'hightide of Buddhism' reached its peak with the recognition of Buddhism as the state religion in 1961. The military junta of General Ne Win which took over power in 1962 rejects Marxism, Western-style democracy and 'the materialism of the so-called leftists';

[1] These comments apply to the Burmese of the 'heartland'; thus as late as 1961 seven regionally-based rebel movements were operating in the other parts of the country—thse included Karen, Shan, Arakanese, Mon, Chinese KMT and White and Red Flag communist groups.

positively it aims to integrate Buddhist ethics with the economic theories of democratic socialism. This seems to parallel developments in Cambodia but is in fact different in essence since in Burma the stability of the internal situation rests upon the counterbalancing of two major forces, those of the Army and of the Buddhist Church.

Partly owing to the problems of containing separatist or regionalist movements but largely as a result of the shortage of Burmese with adequate technical training, the economy has been in a stagnant condition for many years (this in turn, because of the lack of opportunities which is a consequence of stagnation, leads to a steady loss of the more capable Burmese through emigration and thus further aggravates the situation). The economic policies expounded since independence have been policies of an extreme socialist variety but lacking the planning and the mobilisation of the country's resources to make them effective. Much of the legislation has been designed to protect the Burmese from exploitation by outsiders but, since most of the trade is in foreign hands and the Burmese have shown no great enthusiasm for moving into the commercial sector, the effect of this legislation has been simply to stifle trade. And the so-called 'nationalised industries' such as the oil industry are merely industries in which the Burmese government has a 50 per cent share but which otherwise operate in the same conditions as before 'nationalisation' with foreigners providing most of the technical and organisational know-how. The economy under these conditions remains a weak economy and, given the increasing dependence on a small range of exports (in 1938 rice represented 50 per cent of the exports by value, in 1962 75 per cent), an increasingly vulnerable one.

Burma, in short, confronts regionalist or separatist tendencies which menace the very existence of the Burmese state within its present frontiers; it has scarcely begun to confront the problems presented by its 'under-development', problems which, given its economic stagnation and slow but steady population expansion, will become explosive in the years ahead.

(III) THE REPUBLIC OF INDONESIA

The very size of its population puts Indonesia into a class of its own among the nonaligned nations of Southeast Asia; moreover, the country has enjoyed a very considerable measure of prestige as a country which achieved its independence by force of arms from an unwilling colonial power. Indonesia's role in the Bandung Conference set the seal on this prestige; since Bandung Indonesia has pursued a policy of nonalignment with a strong anti-colonial emphasis.

Indonesia's 100 million inhabitants are unevenly distributed over an immense island belt which extends some 3,500 miles from east to west and 1,200 miles from north to south. This island world is a world of immense variety, ranging from wet and heavily forested mountain environments, through marshland environments to environments such as that of Java which, because of its lighter rainfall, lighter forest cover and rich volcanic soils, was particularly attractive to early man. This varied environment was occupied by a great variety of peoples ranging from Negrito and Papuan to Malay and was exposed to a great diversity of cultural influences. This diversity, and the fragmentation by the sea, has contributed to the strong regionalist movements with which the central government has had to contend. At the same time, the sea both separates and unites, and the spread of the Malays from their home zone in the western islands, the rise of the great trading empires of the past and the diffusion of cultural forms such as Hinduism or Islam have been facilitated by the ease of movement across the waters of this Southeast Asian Mediterranean.

Within this 'Mediterranean', control of the seas has always been the key to political power; this was true in the days of the early trading empires—Sri Vijaya and Majapahit—no less than in the days of Portuguese or Dutch domination. Moreover, the sea permitted the rise of a cultural entity, a Malayan entity, which extends beyond the limits of contemporary Indonesia and to which the term 'Greater Indonesia' can be applied. The unity of this Greater Indonesia is based on three major factors. First, the common physiological and cultural characteristics of the major ethnic groups in the region; all belong racially to the same Deutero-Malay group and while a variety of languages is spoken, all are based on Malayo-Polynesian foundation with a form of market Malay serving as a lingua franca. Secondly, the unity of religion; the Malayan-Indonesian bloc represents one of the largest Moslem blocs in the world though within the region, as we have already seen (p. 36), there are many variations on the doctrines of orthodox Islam. Thirdly, the unity imparted by a common way of life, especially wet-rice cultivation which, in the words of Robert Curtis, 'provides the common cultural humus on which the regional "civilisations" form a brilliant, variegated effloration'.

This unity was destroyed by the impact of European colonialism which partitioned the world of 'Greater Indonesia' between Britain and the Netherlands, leaving a relic of the former Portuguese empire in the divided island of Timor. The boundaries of the new colonial empires did not crystallise out immediately (thus during the Napoleonic Wars Java and Sumatra were under British rule) and, like most colonial boundaries, were arbitrary and haphazard, showing little regard for the historical, cultural or economic realities of the area. Nevertheless, they did crystallise out and within the new and arbitrary frontiers the consolidation of colonial administration and its growing penetration in depth created major divergences within what had been a cultural, historical and commercial unity. Comparison between the policies of Britain and the Netherlands in the area illustrate some of the processes at work.[1] In their Malayan territories the British pursued a policy of indirect rule, which strengthened the power of the local Malayan rulers; moreover, economic development was based on the massive importation of indentured Chinese and Indian labour. By contrast, Dutch policy was based on a highly organised system of direct administration which reduced the traditional rulers to the rank of mere salaried officers of the colonial administration. This, as Curtis points out, is closely linked with the Dutch policy of economic exploitation which rested on compulsory cultivation by the Javanese peasant of

[1] For much of what follows I have used Robert Curtis' 'Malaysia and Indonesia' in *New Left Review 28* (1964), pp. 4–32.

selected crops, a system which drew the rural areas into the cash economy and at the same time demanded a vast army of officials if it were to function successfully. But even within the Netherlands Indies there were divergences; Sumatra, for example, was developed late, was administered under an indirect system of government (which lacked, however, the coherence of the Malayan system) and, since it was sparsely inhabited, its economic development depended largely on immigrant labour (Chinese in the tin-mining areas of Bangka and Billiton, Javanese in the estate area around Medan).

As elsewhere in Southeast Asia, the present century witnessed a strong nationalist reaction against colonialism. The major manifestations of this were the foundation in 1912 of the Islamic organisation *Sarekat Islam* and, in 1920, of the Indonesian Communist Party (PKI). The fact that the shattering of the old social structures had been so profound and that rural population pressure coupled with cityward migration had led to social disruption on a large scale gave this reaction an intensity unmatched in the British Malayan territories; by the outbreak of the Second World War the situation was becoming increasingly explosive.

The Japanese occupation had far-reaching effects. It destroyed the old colonial structure and with it the myth of European superiority; it introduced new techniques of mass-control through propaganda; it drew the local nationalist leaders into the highest posts in the administration (even though they were intended as little more than figureheads). But more important than these things were the facts that the Japanese division of the 'Greater Indonesian' area into three military commands ignored the boundaries of the European colonial administration and thus challenged the whole idea of 'natural' frontiers; that the needs of the Japanese administration for a lingua franca expedited the rise of market Malay as a modern national language; that the Japanese organisation of the people of Indonesia gave the emerging Indonesian leaders important lessons in the mobilisation of the masses which could be applied later in the drive for independence. And it is important to stress, for this was to prove of major relevance in the post-independence period, that these Japanese influences, like the earlier Dutch influences, were felt most strongly in Java; this island, because of the political awareness of its people, became the leader of the Indonesian Revolution.

The Indonesian Revolution was both an assertion of national independence and a process of reshaping Indonesian society; the first was achieved after a bitter struggle against the Dutch, the second, as recent events have indicated, is still going on. And as a background to, and a partial explanation of, the changing quality of the Indonesian political scene we have to bear in mind the small size of the *élite* group, the strong regional contrasts and antagonisms, and the personality of President Sukarno, one of the great 'charismatic' leaders of Southeast Asia. The smallness of the *élite* group (a result of Dutch educational policy) and what Curtis describes as its 'curious cohesiveness' (partly the result of marriage within the group) is an important factor making possible abrupt shifts in policy. Perhaps the most striking example of this type of shift is afforded by the contrasts between the early post-revolution period when spokesmen drawn from the *élite* groups of the Outer Islands were dominant and favoured a Western orientation and the period after 1954 when the influence of the Javanese intelligentsia was reflected in an abrupt change in the country's external orientation. This episode draws attention to the second element in the Indonesian political scene—the deep regional-based divisions within Indonesian society. These are partly economic: Sumatra and, to a lesser extent, Celebes and South Borneo, are the main export areas, Java with its dense and heavily urbanised population the great importer. The major rebel areas in the 1957–58 outbreak of rebellion were the wealthier export-surplus areas which sought to by-pass Java and the central government and, by taking trade into their own hands, retain for themselves wealth which would otherwise have flowed towards Java. The contrasts are partly sociological: the strongly developed collective quality of life typical of the closely-packed rice-growing peoples of Java standing opposed to the individualism typical of commercial peasant agriculture in the thinly-settled Outer Islands. They are also partly religious: northern Sumatra, northern Celebes and some of the eastern islands have been Christianised; Orthodox Islam is strongest in parts of Sumatra and Borneo and in West Java; the rest of Java, nominally Moslem, preserves a strong and syncretic Hindu-Buddhist tradition. It is these divisive elements that prompt Curtis' judgement that 'Indonesian society is in many respects a dozen different societies with autonomous lives of their own, linked by the great metropolitan centres (mainly on Java)'. The emergence of Indonesia as a unified state is possible only if this fragmentation can be overcome and it is in this context that the role of Sukarno has been of such critical importance.

Sukarno threw himself into the struggle for Indonesian liberation in the late 'twenties. He spent long years in prison under the Dutch but for the last twenty years has been the dominating figure in the country's political life, a position he owes partly to his oratorical skill, partly to his immense energy, partly to his record as a dedicated revolutionary. This latter has given him the charisma which alone has held Indonesian society together; while the power of the other charismatic leaders of Southeast Asia is derived from the fact that such leaders are the personification of a more or less homogeneous population, Sukarno's power rests on the fact that he alone possessed the ability to maintain a balance between conflicting cliques, conflicting interests and conflicting regional aspirations. And he alone has been able to hold some sort of balance between the two most powerful opposing groups—the Army and the Communist Party—and the priority which has had to be accorded to the maintenance of this balance has meant that the urgent tasks of reconstruction and economic development have had to be shelved. The result has been virtual stagnation, if not deterioration, of the whole Indonesian economy.

Meanwhile, in external policies Indonesia had shifted from an earlier 'triangular' policy in which the nonaligned countries of the Third World were seen as playing a balancing or mediating role between the capitalist West and the communist East, towards a bipolar policy which contrasted the 'new emerging forces' (such as Indonesia) with the 'old-established forces' (the countries of the Western bloc, but including, in the eyes of some Indonesians, the U.S.S.R.). This global vision lay behind the recent policy of 'Confrontation' with

Malaysia (regarded by Indonesia as a 'neo-colonial' structure, hastily erected by Britain, one of the 'old-established forces', to safeguard her interests in Southeast Asia). In the formulation of this policy of confrontation fear of 'Anglosaxon encirclement' had been an important driving force; so, too, were more deeply-rooted elements such as the memory of a greater Indonesia which would embrace all the Malayan territories. Moreover, factional interests served to unite otherwise divergent groups behind the policy; thus the Communist Party supported confrontation because opposition to Malaysia, a neo-colonial creation, gave focus to the Party's revolutionary drive while the Army supported the policy because this undeclared war gave it a new *raison d'être* (the West New Guinea problem being solved) and ensured a high level of priority for the military men's demands on the country's budget.

At the moment of writing, however, the divisive forces in Indonesian society (and notably the more reactionary Islamic elements) have reasserted themselves, backed perhaps by outside forces, and are destroying the precarious equilibrium Sukarno has maintained. This swing to the right has been accompanied by a massive slaughter of so-called 'Communist sympathisers' in parts of Java and by an apparent breakdown of the economy, leading to widespread deaths from starvation in some of the Outer Islands such as Lombok. The contours of the immediate future are as yet unclear. What *does* seem clear, however, is that the policy of relying on external aid to solve its administrative and economic problems which the new régime seems to be inclining towards offers no long-term solution to Indonesia's problems. Confrontation has now ended, Indonesia is rejoining the world community of nations and rebuilding her links with the West. But nothing in the way of a final solution to the country's problems has been achieved; rather has the day of reckoning merely been put off for the time being. And when the country *does* confront the problem of rebuilding its shattered economy and re-establishing that unity for which Sukarno has struggled, the politicians may find the problem insuperably aggravated by the cumulative bitterness left behind by recent events. They may find also that, stripped of all its verbiage, Sukarno's assessment of

Indonesia's position in the world and its role in a Third World context may yet prove to be more accurate than it is at present fashionable (or in Indonesia safe) to admit.

(B) The Western-aligned Countries of Southeast Asia

The countries discussed in the preceding sections are countries which are politically nonaligned (a position which does not exclude a measure of hostility to an often tactless West) and socialist in their political and economic systems, though this socialism is indigenous in character and has little in common with the classical socialism of the West or, for that matter, the Soviet Union.

The second group of nations may be described as the Western-aligned nations—or the satellites of the West. These two alternative labels remind us that the political geography of Southeast Asia can be interpreted in two ways—from a Western viewpoint or from an Asian viewpoint; what we see, what labels we apply to countries, depends largely upon the viewpoint we adopt. Yet if we as geographers are to reach any real understanding of this complex and fragmented Southeast Asian world we must at times project ourselves out of our own society and endeavour to see the world we seek to interpret as it appears to other, non-Western, peoples. It need hardly be stressed that the world as seen from Hanoi, Djakarta or from Phnom Penh seems a very different world from that we see from London, Washington or Sydney.

Seen from a Western viewpoint the nations in this group are elements in a military and political structure designed to 'contain' communism and especially Chinese communism. Only Thailand and the Philippines are formal members of SEATO but South Vietnam is regarded as under the SEATO 'umbrella'; Malaysia–Singapore is tied in to the Anglo-American defence system in Southeast Asia while Laos, in theory neutral, is in fact a microcosm of the Cold War—the nothern provinces are held by a regionally-based communist movement (the Pathet Lao) while the capital, Vientiane, is effectively under American control. Economically, all these countries have been the recipients of considerable military and economic aid though, since a good deal of this has found its way into the pockets of the *élite* groups, there has not been a corresponding degree of economic development. Indeed, external aid, coupled with the tendency to uneven development which is a characteristic of the free enterprise system, has tended to widen the gap between city and country and has aggravated social instability.

Seen from the viewpoint adopted by many Asians the situation appears rather different. Malaysia is, in their eyes, an artificial structure designed to safeguard and to perpetuate the British economic and military presence in the region. Thailand and the Philippines are regarded simply as Western satellites, complaisant partners in the implementation of Western policies in Southeast Asia. South Vietnam is regarded as a country which, in everything but name, is a colonial appendage of the United States, and where the latter are attempting to perpetuate a division of the Vietnamese lands which, as the Geneva accords laid down, was to be a temporary division designed to facilitate a military regrouping. Laos is a country where external intervention has torn the state asunder and where massive financial aid has merely created a new—and dependent—privileged group without solving any of the country's economic difficulties. And all these types of Western intervention—military, political or economic—are seen as devices to consolidate and prolong the West's control over the Pacific margins of Asia.

The truth may lie somewhere between these two points of view; what is important, however, if we wish to understand Southeast Asia today, is to strive to see some of its problems not solely through the eyes of Western observers, but also through the eyes of its own peoples.

The countries we shall consider in this section show a great diversity—in population, in degree of ethnic homogeneity, in the level of their economic development. They are alike in other respects: in each country economic development (if there is any, which is doubtful in Laos) is taking place within a free-enterprise system and this, largely because of its single-minded preoccupation with maximising profits, results in an extremely patchy pattern of development. There has been little attempt to mobilise their greatest resource—their manpower—for this would involve a measure of state intervention and planning incompatible with economic liberalism; instead, foreign loans, foreign aid and profit-oriented foreign capital keep their budgets in some sort of equilibrium. They are countries in which there has been little structural change in society, which means that the agrarian problem, in the shape of a predatory landlord group or unequal distribution of cropland, is important on the national or regional scale. And in their external policies they are either active participants in, or passive supporters of, Western policies in Southeast Asia.

(*I*) *MALAYSIA–SINGAPORE*

The formerly British sector of the 'Greater Indonesian' region, the territories of Malaya, Singapore and Borneo which made up the edifice known as Malaysia, consists of a diversity of landscapes and of human regions, a complexity of local and immigrant peoples thrown together by Western man's search for markets and exploitable raw materials. Indeed, it is no exaggeration to claim that these British Malaysian territories offer what is perhaps the most striking single example to be found anywhere of the way in which the commercial impact of an expanding Europe *created* the geography and the socio-economic problems of a dependent territory.

In mainland Malaya the economic development of the late nineteenth and early twentieth centuries, centring on rubber and tin-mining, created a series of plantation or mining enclaves whose market-oriented economy stood out in sharp contrast to the subsistence economies of the rest of the peninsula. This development created a very large demand for labour and this was met by the import of indentured labourers from China and India; the numbers of these were sufficient in some areas to swamp the local Malay population. These changes affected the country unevenly; they were largely confined to the western coastal strip and had little direct impact on the north or on the eastern half of Malaya. They were thus responsible for the emergence of what is today the basic contrast within the Malay peninsula, the contrast between Old Malaya and New Malaya.

Old Malaya is the northernmost part of Malaya; it is what

may be termed the 'Malay home zone', the area of densest Malay settlement and an area little touched by the immigration of Chinese or Indians. It has also been little touched by the economic developments which have transformed the west coast strip; the population is concerned largely with subsistence, food-getting activities, and some two-thirds to three-quarters of the total are engaged in rice-growing. Agriculture is not notably efficient, the landlord takes a considerable share of the peasants' crop as rent and the population has tended to remain poor and backward. As in many other poor and backward peasant areas its people's politics tend to be conservative, if not reactionary; it is the chief stronghold of the reactionary and sectionalist Pan-Malayan Islamic Party.

New Malaya stands in complete contrast. This is, broadly, western and southern Malaya, the area which has been most affected by Western economic development in the last two or three generations. This is the area where the development of an export economy based on tin and rubber called into being an urban infrastructure and a dense transport network unparalleled in Old Malaya, the area where the labour demands associated with Western economic development led to massive imports of Chinese and Indian labour. Today this is multiracial Malaya, the part of the country where the Malays (many of whom are relatively recent immigrants from Indonesia) make up less than one-third of the total population. And in the cities and the mining districts and plantations of the area politics have a radical quality totally lacking in the politics of traditional Malaya or Old Malaya.

And, in addition to these two major regions created by the uneven impact of the West, and offering a striking contrast to both, there is another Malaya. This is 'indigenous' or 'aboriginal' Malaya, the Malaya inhabited by forest peoples such as the Semang or Sakai, groups pushed into the interior by the Malays, little touched by later outside influences, but occupying some two-thirds of the country.

Finally, soldered on as it were to the tip of Malaya, the city of Singapore, 'the last and greatest of a long line of Southeast Asian city states', a city founded some five generations ago on a thinly settled island and which today, with its suburbs, has a population of $1\frac{3}{4}$ millions. It rose to importance as a collecting centre for the region's raw material exports and as a distributing centre for Western imported manufactures and its commercial influence extended over much of the Indonesian world. It was from the beginning a largely Chinese city; in 1965 it broke with the Federation and became independent, becoming thus, after the Chinese People's Republic and Taiwan, a 'Third China'.

The Malayan Federation, still more the Federation of Malaysia, exhibits a diversity of landscapes, of human regions, a complexity of peoples thrown together by Western man's search for markets and exploitable raw materials. In the words of Han Suyin, 'Chinese, Malay, Indians, three words, three sweeping generalisations out of which it has been planned to create a country called Malaya, a single people to be called Malayans'. And, as the last few years have indicated, it is an uneasy and explosive complexity of peoples.

The problems both Malaya and the succeeding Federation of Malaysia face arise from the area's colonial past; they are the communal (or 'racial') problem and the economic problem posed by a warped and dependent economy faced with accommodating a rapidly growing labour force.

The communal problem is essentially one of creating a viable and coherent state from three very disparate elements—a rural-based, almost feudal Malay community and two geographically-localised and highly cash-conscious immigrant communities, the Chinese and the Indians. Initial attempts at nation-building foundered on this problem and it took the weariness and disillusion of a long civil war before an effective Chinese–Malay partnership began to emerge. This was the Alliance party which has governed the country since it became independent in 1957; it is an uneasy partnership, however, for the two strongest elements are represented by the wealthy Chinese capitalist group and the more feudal elements in Malay society. The voting system has been heavily loaded in the direction of the Malay rural voter; even this, however, has not prevented the emergence of a reactionary, strongly communal party, the Pan-Malayan Islamic Party which got over one-fifth of the votes in the 1959 elections. Recent years, during which the Malays have consolidated their political position, have seen little diminution in the strength of communal feeling. There are signs, indeed, that this may increase and that, in the absence of large-scale economic development, Malaya will become increasingly polarised, with, at one extreme, the impoverished, backward, and religion-dominated Malay peasantry of the north, at the other, the diverse, and more radically-oriented populations of the mining and plantation areas of southern and western Malaya. The concentration of much of Malaya's economic development in relatively limited areas of the West coast has contributed in this direction, to a widening gap between Old and New Malaya and between the various communities who jostle one another in peninsular Malaya.

The other British territories in Southeast Asia—Singapore and the Borneo territories—consist of a scattered group of territories, individually economically weak, politically vulnerable, and, except for Singapore, possessing relatively small populations. Trade between these countries represented one-third of their total trade in 1960 so some measure of economic integration had already emerged; closer formal political association, it seemed, would bring more advantages: it would double the size of the market, encourage the development of new industries and the larger and more diversified economy would be more likely to attract foreign investment than the individual territory. These possible economic advantages were important in the rise of the Federation of Malaysia; even more important were the advantages from the communal point of view (which in this context means the *Malay* point of view) and the military advantages. As far as the communal aspect is concerned, the wider Federation offered the opportunity of building up a sizeable 'indigenous' block, consisting of Malays and other groups such as the Dayaks, who would make up slightly over two-fifths of the total population and outnumber the Chinese group, thus neutralising the threat of a radical Chinese Singapore. As for the military aspect, Federation was designed to stabilise the British position in the region (thus safeguarding both the important base at Singapore and the very considerable British investments in Malaya) and, by the transformation of the British Borneo territories from colonies to parts of a self-governing federation, would give a new and definitive character to the colonial carving-up of Borneo between the former Dutch and British colonial empires. It was this implied 'definitive' solution to the Borneo question, together with the fear that the Federation was part of an 'Anglosaxon' scheme to encircle Indonesia[1] which threw the latter country into active opposition to the whole Federation concept.

The economic and political arguments for integrating *Singapore* into a wider Malaysian unity were very strong; in the words of Lee Kuan-yew '[Malaya] is the hinterland which produces the rubber and tin that keep our shop-window economy going. It is the base that made Singapore the capital city. Without this economic base Singapore would not survive.' In spite of this, the communal tensions between the dominantly Chinese and 'radical' city state of Singapore and the growing and increasingly conservative anti-Chinese Malay nationalism based on Kuala Lumpur proved too strong and in 1965 Singapore broke away from the Federation to become an independent state. The future of the state will be dependent on regional trade and this includes trade with Indonesia which has always played a major role in Singapore's economy; under such conditions Singapore has a very real interest in the normalisation of relations, especially commercial relations with Indonesia.

The extension of the concept of Malaysia to embrace the *British Borneo territories* is to be seen against the background of communal tensions, above all the fear of the Malays that they would be outnumbered by Chinese. In a federation embracing Malaya and Singapore 3·7 million 'Malaysians' would be balanced against 3·8 million Chinese. If, however, the Borneo territories were included in a wider Federation the addition of sizeable non-Chinese populations reduced the relative weight of the Chinese community considerably—to 4·2 million out of a total population of 9·8 million. It was this preoccupation with the communal situation which encouraged the Malay drive to

[1] With American influence still dominant in the Philippines to the east, an Australia with uncertain attitudes to the south, and American and British sea or air power dominant over much of the area a pro-Anglosaxon Malaysia would complete the 'encirclement'.

bring about a wider grouping; Malay interests coincided with British imperial interests and the enlarged Federation of Malaysia came into existence in 1963. Some 1¼ million inhabitants of British Borneo (out of a total population of 5¼ million for Indonesian and British Borneo combined) were added to the Federation of Malaya and Singapore; the table below gives the racial composition of the new Federation of Malaysia:

TABLE 6

Population of Malaysia, 1960 (000s)

	Malays	*Chinese*	*Indians & Pakistanis*	*Borneo Indigenous*	*Others*	*Total*
Federation	3,461*	2,552	773	—	123	6,909
Singapore	227*	1,231	138	—	38	1,634
Sarawak	129	229	2	378	6	744
N. Borneo	25	105	3	283	39†	455
TOTAL	3,842	4,117	916	661	206	9,742

*Includes persons of Indonesian origin now largely absorbed into Malay community.

† Of whom five-eighths were Indonesians.

The withdrawal of Singapore underlines the force of the strong tensions behind the Federal façade. Moreover, even in its initial stages the move towards federation aggravated rather than reduced communal suspicions in the Borneo territories; the emergence in Sarawak of the S.U.P.P. (Sarawak United Peoples Party), a largely Chinese party, was followed by the emergence of similar communal-based political parties among the non-Chinese, thus creating a strong political polarisation of the society along ethnic lines. And, if the Borneo indigenous groups are suspicious of the economic and potential political power of the Chinese, they are no less suspicious of the motives of the Malay-dominated central government. Even without a hostile Indonesia on her Bornean frontier the long-term prospects for the Federation are unpromising.

(*II*) *REPUBLIC OF THE PHILIPPINES*

The Republic of the Philippines has a complex and sometimes contradictory personality. The country can boast of the earliest nationalist movement in Asia (headed by Jose Rizal in the 1890s) though this nationalist movement was at an early stage taken over by the land-owning groups, the *caciques*. It is the only Christian nation in Southeast Asia, claims to be the third largest English-speaking nation in the world and is today, in the words of Victor Purcell, 'the westernmost extension of the American Empire of the Pacific'. In spite of two decades of independence it remains economically heavily dependent on the U.S.A. (see Figure 27) and is institutionally closely tied in to the U.S. business economy; this dependence is reflected in the nation's international stance—as one American writer puts it, 'the Philippines regularly has stood as a dependable ally with the United States despite criticism from some more neutralist-oriented Asian neighbours'. Yet though the Spanish and American periods isolated them from the rest of Southeast Asia Filipinos consider themselves a Southeast Asian people, a 'Malay' people, and this identification may be expected to increase in strength as Filipino nationalism becomes more coherent and as the geographical and cultural obstacles to integration are overcome.

These obstacles are numerous. There is the physical obstacle posed by the fragmentation of the nation into some 7,000 islands; many are isolated so that the 'cultural gradient' between, for example, the Batanes island group of northern Luzon and metropolitan Manila is as steep as any in Asia. There is the ethnic barrier posed by the fragmentation of the Filipino people into some 75 main linguistic groups and over 150 languages and dialects; it is true that the 'minority groups' make up only one-tenth of the total population but many of these—the composite group known as the Igorots, the nomadic mountain tribes of Luzon, the Islamised 'Moros' of Mindanao—present major problems of assimilation or integration. There is the sociological barrier posed by the tradition of an intense family loyalty which transcends with difficulty the limits of a group larger than the family. There is the legacy of colonialism which produced a minimum of geographic and political integration which might serve as a basis for Filipino nationalism; which, indeed, aggravated existing divergences and created new ones, illustrated by the widening gap between an overcrowded countryside and a parasitic capital city or by the emergence of powerful pressure groups within the Filipino Congress.

The historical and cultural complexity which constitutes the dominant element in the geography of the country have been summarised by J. E. Spencer: 'The people are attracted to the Occident, tied by bonds to the Orient and threatened by the advance of what aspires to be the Soviet world. The islands and their population are chiefly agricultural, chiefly rural, chiefly literate, chiefly Christian and politically sophisticated, but each term misleads into overgeneralisation. An urban resident might wish to add the phrase, chiefly capitalistic; but a rural critic would certainly counter with the phrase, pre-capitalistic. Heterogeneity—the intermixture of diverse elements and trends in the economy and culture of the Philippines—is far more prevalent than unity and conformity. Two very different patterns of treatment by Spain and the United States, ending in voluntarily given independence, have left deep marks.'

The Americans took over the Philippines, after defeating Spain, at the end of the nineteenth century. Their administration was strongly paternalistic but this did not stifle the Filipino drive for national independence; from the establishment of the first legislative assembly in 1907 until 1946 the *Nacionalista* party (largely landlord-based but nationalist in its orientation) was in power. The country achieved independence as a 'commonwealth' in 1936 and became fully independent a decade later. However, during the generation and a half of American control the Filipino economy had become closely integrated with that of the United States which provided the major market for Filipino exports and whose businessmen had built up an important complex of interests in the islands. Under such conditions, behind a façade of political independence, the Filipino economy remained a dependent economy and the possibilities of creating an autonomous national economy were further limited by legislative measures which put United States businessmen on a basis of equality with local entrepreneurs. The first early years of independence were dominated by Manuel Roxas and the Liberal Party; the administration contained a high proportion of politicians who had collaborated with the Japanese (including Roxas himself) and who were less preoccupied with the interests of the nation than with exploiting for their own benefit the massive flow of American aid. The result was an increasingly sharp polarisation of society between a wealthy and corrupt ruling class and the great mass of the impoverished, and, geographically, a sharpening of the contrasts between metropolitan Manila, one of the most striking examples of a parasitic city in Southeast Asia, and the countryside condemned to poverty by an iniquitous land tenure system. The peasant war known as the Huk rebellion represented a violent reaction to this situation. The programme of the Huks has been set out concisely by Victor Purcell: 'In addition to the continuance of the agrarian problem, they attributed the misfortunes of the Philippines to "American militarism", and aimed at securing a state of affairs in which the islands would cut all its economic, political and military links with the former Metropolitan Power. Added to this they urged . . . the purchase of the great estates and their resale to their bona-fide tenants; the provision of houses for the masses; the abolition of the tenancy system and its replacement by that of leasehold; the disbandment of the civil guard; the recognition of the guerrillas and of the rights of citizens to bear arms; and the adoption of a plan for social security and minimum wages.'

Like similar reformist or revolutionary programmes in mainland Southeast Asia (e.g. that of the Viet Minh) the programme has a strong social content; at the same time, it has its roots firmly in the agrarian structure. This is the 'Achilles heel' of the whole Filipino situation. It is true that the American administration had largely liquidated the immense holdings of the Church and had encouraged homesteading on public lands; nevertheless, these developments were largely offset by the expansion of population, by the extension of large-scale cash crop production which led to a concentration of land ownership and an increase in farm labour and in tenant farming at the expense of small independent peasant holdings. Thus, while the population of the Philippines increased 60 per cent in the inter-war years, the number of farms *decreased* by 16 per cent; a large class of landless families came into existence. According to the 1948 Census of Agriculture almost half the farms, occupying less than two-fifths of the farm area, were operated by tenants or part-tenants. The proportion of tenant-operated farms is highest in the oldest-settled areas, the areas which produce largely for market; in Central Luzon, the rice-granary of the Philippines, it ranges from 88 per cent to 63 per cent according to district. Most of such holdings are operated on a share-cropping system (*kasama*), the crop being divided 50 : 50 between the land-owner and the tenant. Yields are low, for the peasant lives so close to the margin of existence he cannot afford to risk innovations and the whole system inhibits improvement. The burden of indebtedness is high (over 90 per cent of the peasants in Central Luzon, for example, are in debt); interest rates range between 66 per cent and 200 per cent per annum. The major indices of the peasants sub-human existence have been listed by Tsutomu Takigawa: 'their humble nipa huts; poor clothes; a monotonous and scanty diet which invariably consists of rice and dried fish; chronic undernourishment; many endemic diseases; wide-spread tuberculosis; boils and ulcerated legs. . . .' It is not surprising that it is these areas of tenant farming which have been the areas most affected by agrarian unrest and violence. And, as in many parts of the under-developed world, the wealth accruing to the land-owning group from this exploitation is not invested in forms which might benefit the economy; rather is it hoarded, invested in real estate, or spent in maintaining an excessively high level of life.

The Huk rebellion which grew out of these conditions was broken, partly by overwhelming military force (backed by the United States), partly by promises of reform on the part of President Magsaysay. However, to promise reform was one thing, to carry it through a landlord-dominated Congress was an entirely different matter. Magsaysay's reforms were emasculated by landlord-interests in the Philippines Congress and, as F. H. Golay puts it, 'effective land reform is still ahead in the Philippines'. The result has been a continuation of agrarian unrest and a resurgence, on a small but significant scale, of guerrilla activity.

One of the indirect results of the war against the Huks was the introduction of emergency measures to safeguard the deteriorating Filipino economy. These included strict economic controls such as the limitation of imports and restrictions on the remittance of profits overseas. These measures contributed to the growth and the entrenchment of Filipino industrial and manufacturing interests and the emergence of a national bourgeoisie whose interests conflict with the older-established American interests in the Philippines. This group has visions of an industrialised Philippines dominating the Southeast Asian region and acting as a processor of local raw materials. It is a group possessing great wealth and political influence and while it has precious little sympathy for movements such as the Huk movement it too is an agent of social and political change. Thus Filipino society is being subjected to socio-political pressures at both its base and its summit.

One of the major results of lack of any planning and especially of any welfare planning has been the increasing and dangerous concentration of wealth, in terms of class and in spatial terms. Thus, the 4 per cent or so who fall in the managerial and administrative groups enjoy a median weekly income some six times as high as the 61 per cent who fall in the farming category; the population of Manila has an average income two and a half times as high as the average for the Philippines and some four times as high as the income of the population of Ilocos and Mountain Province, or the province of East Visayas. It is social and economic inequalities of this type, added to the tensions arising from a repressive agrarian situation and aggravated by a very rapid expansion of population, which give a dangerously explosive quality to the whole Filipino situation.

(*III*) *THAILAND*

Thailand is unique in that it alone of the Southeast Asian states succeeded in preserving its independence during the European colonial partition of the region. This has meant that some of the problems—and the attitudes—typical of its Asian neighbours who are emerging from colonialism have little meaning in Thailand; the country has tended to stand aloof from some of the currents of change which are transforming much of the rest of Asia, so much aloof, indeed, that one Thai has described his country as 'a misplaced European country'. At the same time, colonialism *did* have an impact for, until the European period, the boundaries of the state had remained vague and fluid; as a political unit Thailand was defined largely by the competing expansionisms of France and Britain. The western and southern frontiers were thus defined largely as a result of British policy in Burma and Malaya; the northern and eastern frontiers took shape as a result of French pressure. As J. E. Spencer comments perceptively: 'Thailand is far more a politico-historical phenomenon than a cultural one'.

That real territorial stability has not yet been found is suggested by the progressive rearrangement of the state's administrative pattern; in the words of Spencer: 'Thai operation of their geographical territory has not yet found stable regional bases on which to establish administrative patterns'. In part this is rooted in the dichotomy of the country, in the contrast, typical of Southeast Asia, between the dominant culture, which is lowland-based, and the many minority cultures occupying the upland margins. The key area, as in Burma, is the central lowland, the plain of the Menam. This is the area of most compact Thai settlement and the most important area agriculturally. In the extreme south of peninsular Thailand there is a sizeable Malay population; in the west and northwest hill country Karen, Shan and Wa-Palaung peoples overlap from Burma into Thailand; in the north groups such as the Miao and Yao represent extensions of the upland groups of South China; towards the Mekong there is no meaningful frontier separating the Thai and the Laotian Thai. It is true that it is claimed that some 85 per cent of the country's population consists of Thais (a figure which must include, it seems, a sizeable proportion of the Sino-Thai group), nevertheless the area occupied by minority groups is large, strategically situated close to Thailand's sensitive frontier regions, and poorly integrated into the larger political unit of which it forms part. And the economic stagnation of these remoter regions by comparison with the core area of the Lower Menam tends if anything to widen the gap between the minority regions and the rest of Thailand.

Like other Southeast Asian countries Thailand experimented with democracy on the Western pattern but with little success. Recent years have, therefore, been characterised by the search for 'a political system based on Thai traditions of authority'; this trend towards an authoritarian rule was typified by the emergence of Field-Marshal Sarit as virtual dictator. Sarit's rise followed a period when corruption and general discontent were widespread; against such a background many were prepared to accept his judgement that parliamentary systems of government in Thailand were a failure, or at least premature, and accepted his drastic policy of abolishing all political parties, the National Assembly and the constitution, and establishing an outright military dictatorship. An appointed Constituent Assembly was set up in 1959 but martial law remained in effect, all political parties were banned and the press controlled. The later stages of Sarit's régime were marked by an increasingly close collaboration between the dictator and the monarchy, by a stabilisation (at least superficially) of internal conditions and by a measure of economic development. On Sarit's death in 1963 he was succeeded by Field-Marshal Thanan Kittacachorn. There was no major change in internal policies; as far as external policies are concerned, the long-held view of Thai leaders—'that their small nation can best avoid foreign domination in a dangerous world by adjusting its policy to the prevailing power situation'—continued to prevail. This had meant accommodation with Britain and Japan in the past; today it means accommodation with the United States though if the latter power cannot or will not resist communism in Asia there seems little doubt that this pro-American stance would be called into question.

The rate of economic growth in recent years (a 6–7 per cent growth in National Income per annum) has been impressive. Longer term perspectives, however, reveal major problems, of which the most important are those of developing the country before the population becomes either too poor or too numerous and of correcting the excessive concentration of wealth and development in the Bangkok area. The country is undergoing a period of rapid population growth (3 per cent per annum) which will boost its present population of 30 million to 50 million by 1982; 46 per cent of these will be under 15 years of age so that the burden of dependency will be a heavy one. Over the same period the *per capita* income, at present slightly over £30 (1,806 *baht*), may be expected to increase some 50 per cent. As in many 'under-developed' countries, however, such average figures mean very little; indeed one of the basic problems Thailand faces is the gross disparity in the pattern of incomes as a result of which a very small minority—in banking, trade, construction and investment—monopolise a high proportion of the national wealth. These groups are predominantly based in Bangkok and their increasing affluence, set against the relative stagnation of the agricultural sector, creates in Thailand a dangerous social—and political—situation.

Much of the country's economic growth has been due to this inflation of the tertiary sector. Industry has contributed less to the national economy than might have been expected and the relative importance of agriculture's contribution to the G.N.P. has dropped from one-half in 1951 to one-third in 1963. The rate of growth in the agricultural sector appears to be of the order of 3 per cent per annum, which means it is just about keeping pace with population growth. This low agricultural productivity is a limiting factor as far as industry based on agricultural raw materials is concerned, while the resulting low incomes of a large proportion of the population means that there is in any case only a limited market for local manufactured goods.

These economic features are closely related to some of the weaknesses of the Thai political situation. The relatively undeveloped character of the secondary sector of the economy has led to the absence of any strong and articulate middle class on which an effective party system might be based. Thailand's large Chinese community (probably some 3½ million strong) comes closest to constituting a middle class though the majority of these are still regarded with suspicion and classed as 'aliens'. Moreover, the weaknesses of the economy are most evident in those areas which are still imperfectly integrated into the Thai state—the areas inhabited by minority peoples; economic differentials thus reinforce ethnic contrasts and suspicions . . . These critical areas include the northeast (which contains one-third of Thailand's population) where rice yields are only one-half the average for Thailand, where drought is a serious problem and the level of rural indebtedness high; here the absence of any clearly defined ethnic frontier with Laos and the presence of a sizeable North Vietnamese community add to the central Government's fear of infiltration. A second critical area is the southern section of Peninsular Thailand; here there is a considerable Malay and Chinese population, politically sophisticated and acutely aware of the failure of the Thai economy to measure up to the level of development (and economic opportunity) across the frontier in Malaya. In this area it is, for example, estimated that rubber yields could be trebled and the area under the crop doubled.

The much-publicised possibility of a threat to the stability of the Thai state as a result of foreign infiltration of these depressed and 'permeable' border zones has led the Thai government and its American allies to devote a good deal of attention—manifesting itself in funds and personnel—to these hitherto neglected border areas. The threat may well be exaggerated[1] for reasons of political expediency (it ensures, for example, a continuing high level of aid) and, as one writer puts it: 'With or without the presence of subversion, however, the threat of discontentment which broods on Thailand's borders would remain the same—the inevitable consequence of a (hitherto) ineffective government in increasingly depressed and historically remote lands.' The threat ensures a continuation of Thailand's pro-Western policy but the extent to which the government can resist 'subversion' (which may be merely another name for the growing intolerance of the peasantry for the seemingly endless stagnation in which they are bogged down) depends largely on economic development and on the reduction of the excessive differentials in economic progress

[1] The 'Thailand Independence Movement' which is Peking-backed was created in 1964, the 'Thailand Patriotic Front' early in 1965. As in South Vietnam, external support of revolutionary movements such as these does not exclude a strong measure of local support.

and levels of living between, on one hand, the 'pole of development' represented by Bangkok, on the other, the rural back-country, whether its people be Thai or minority in their culture. In this close association between political stability, economic development and the widening economic and social gap between capital city and countryside Thailand is a microcosm of the 'under-developed' world as a whole.

(IV) LAOS

There can be few countries whose national unity is as tenuous as that of the tiny Southeast Asian state of Laos. The emergence of the country as an independent state is recent; its physical build—a zone of wild and broken upland country flanked to the west and the south by the valley lands of the Mekong—militates against unity; its corridor location has resulted in a population which is a patchwork of ethnic groups; over much of the country the peasantry remain little aware of complications such as the concept of a Lao state and conscious only of the more immediate forms of grouping such as the family or the village. And modern economic development has done little to integrate the diverse peoples and diverse regions of the country; over wide areas transport is non-existent, the economy is a self-sufficient one, money is used only in the towns and beyond the accessible areas of the Mekong valley in the west the influence of the outside world remains of the slightest. Perhaps the best index to the almost complete lack of any modern infrastructure is given by the fact that in 1960 the country had no railways, two doctors, three engineers and 700 telephones.

The country constitutes a 'corridor zone' between China to the north and the Indochinese lands to the south; if the strategic significance of this position is exaggerated by Western military observers (an exaggeration which accounts for the disproportionate amount of military aid lavished on the country) the position has nevertheless been an important factor in the evolution of the extremely complex ethnic pattern, for it has throughout history exposed this borderland to waves of migrating people. Today, the dominant group, the Lao represent barely half of the country's reputed population;[1] the

[1] Estimated variously at between two million and five million.

remaining groups consist of tribal Thai (15 per cent) and Kha and other related Mon-Khmer peoples making up some thirty different minority groups. There is little tradition of an earlier cultural and political unity to compare with that of the Khmer Empire in Cambodia and during the last three centuries the country was a chaos of little principalities and disputed tribal areas. This fragmentation continued under the French and, when the latter withdrew, the absence of any effective national leadership and the external support given by various Great Powers to competing groups among the small Laotian *élite* led to a chaos of opposing factions whose programmes and whose ambitions had little meaning to the illiterate and malaria-ridden masses.

The last decade has been one long series of shifts and movements, of conflicts and agreements between a small number of individuals and cliques, each with outside support and often with little reference to any community of forces or interests among the Laotian people themselves. Economic development has been virtually non-existent and the attempts by the Americans to stabilise a right-wing and pro-Western régime by lavish aid programmes led merely to corruption, inflation and new gradients of wealth within the country and so played into the hands of the extreme left, the Pathet Lao. With everyone in the capital apparently benefiting from aid and with the rural masses getting nothing, disaffection and a growing receptiveness to communist propaganda spread. The West failed to impose a right-wing government; communist control of the northeast became consolidated; and the coalition government of Prince Souvanna Phouma, a coalition of as unlikely and incompatible groups as can be found anywhere in Southeast Asia, is ostensibly committed to a neutralist policy, Laos meanwhile presents the not unusual picture of a country in which a strong rural-based left-wing movement is in effective control of a sizeable sector of the state's territory and is balanced by right-wing elements who are backed by a 'national' army financed largely by American aid.

Such a situation inhibits both real economic development and the creation of the infrastructure—the transport, the technicians—which would make possible the exploitation of the country's agricultural and mineral resources. These resources include one of the most important deposits of iron ore in Asia—those of Xieng Khouang. Yet the *full* extent of the country's agricultural and mineral potential is still largely unknown: 'Some of the planners say that even now there is so much ignorance about the geography of the country that they do not even know which areas it would most profit the country to open up.' But even the fragmentary information we *do* have suggests that Laos has the resources, both agricultural and mineral, to support a diversified economy, that its present poverty could be eliminated by a dedicated and nation-wide development drive.

Meanwhile, the precarious character of the economy is emphasised by spiralling inflation,[1] falling agricultural output and an increasing dependence on food imports from Thailand. Imports in 1963 were, in terms of value, some forty times the country's exports while, in 1959–60, the civil budget was underwritten to the extent of 65 per cent by foreign grants; of the rest, three-quarters came from customs duties on imports, these latter purchased with aid funds. The tasks confronting the régime are thus immense, the country's potential largely neglected. The evaluation of this potential and the initiation of genuine economic development (for which a realistic but unimplemented plan has been worked out) depends desperately on a period of peace and stability and this cannot be ensured without the good-will of the great powers of both the Western and communist bloc. To that extent the future of Laos is intimately bound up with the broader question of East–West relations.

(*V*) *THE REPUBLIC OF VIETNAM* (*South Vietnam*)

The existence of South Vietnam as a separate political unit can be regarded as one of the more unfortunate results of the Cold War and, above all, of American policy towards China. French rule in the Vietnamese lands was terminated by the Geneva Agreements of 1954; these provided, among other things, for a *temporary* partition of Vietnam along the line of the

[1] Consumer price index for a Laotian family (1959 = 100) reached 473 in Vientiane and 819 in Luang Prabang (March 1964).

17th parallel. This 'partition' was to facilitate military regrouping of the French and Vietnamese forces and was not in any way intended as a permanent settlement; free elections to bring about reunification were to be held in 1956. Largely as a result of the opposition of the Diem régime in South Vietnam (backed by the United States) these elections were never held and what had been originally a purely temporary divide between North and South became a critical frontier along which American military power came into increasingly open confrontation with the East Asian communist bloc. South Vietnam, under the protection of SEATO, became 'a bastion of the free world', a critically important link in the chain of military satellites, running from South Korea through Taiwan, the Philippines, and South Vietnam to Thailand in the west, with which the U.S.A. sought to 'contain' the imagined expansion of People's China.

Yet in terms of the history of the preceding two millennia, in terms of geography, in terms of the sentiments of the Vietnamese people themselves, the Vietnamese lands constitute a single unit. It is a unit forged by the slow and steady expansion of the Vietnamese people from their cradle area in Tonkin down the coast plains of Annam into the delta country of Cochin China; it is a unit containing strong elements of cultural diversity such as the contrast and opposition between lowland Vietnamese and upland tribal people in both North and South, the contrast between the closely settled 'home zone' of Tonkin and the areas of more recent and less close settlement in the far South, the contrast (sharpened during the colonial period) between the food-deficit, mineral-rich North and the food-surplus, mineral-deficient South. These regional contrasts are strong, yet they are perhaps less *contrasts* than *variations* on a single theme; moreover, they pale into insignificance when set against the strong sense of national identity which emerged from almost a thousand years of struggles with China and almost a century of opposition to French colonialism.

It is above all in the countryside and among the peasant masses that the greatest strength of this Vietnamese nationalism is rooted. This was clearly illustrated by the First Indochinese War and is at this moment being underlined by the events of the Second Indochinese War. In both cases Western military power seemed overwhelming and the West (France, then the United States) held most of what seemed to be the key-points—the cities and the communications centres—in an iron grasp. Nevertheless, Vietnamese nationalism, deeply rooted in a closely-knit peasant society remained, and remains, unbroken; it can indeed, be shattered only by the total destruction of the rural society which nourishes it. . . .

The urban population is of relatively limited numerical importance. Partly this may be a result of French colonial policy which, in contrast to British policy in India, stood in the way of the emergence of a significant middle-class group. These city-folk—merchants, administrators, intellectuals, moulded after the fashions of Paris or Washington—have tended to play a conservative role in Vietnamese life. The cities were thus the main bases of French economic and military control in the past as today they are the last bases of American power. The traditional picture, which contrasts the conservatism of the peasantry with the progressive, even revolutionary, quality of the urban *élite* thus has no validity in Vietnam for the roles are reversed.

This drive for change in the countryside (which provides much of the motive force behind the guerrilla war being waged by the National Liberation Front) is rooted in the agrarian system of South Vietnam. This is characterised on the one hand, by a great concentration of land in the hands of a few, on the other, by a great mass of peasants who are either landless or whose plots were too small to support them. In the Annam coast strip 30 per cent of the peasants had no land, 65 per cent had less than half a hectare, while 0·058 per cent of the population held 10 per cent of the land. In the provinces south and west of Saigon Pierre Gourou states that two out of three peasant families were landless; almost 50 per cent of the land was held by one-fiftieth of the population. Added to this is the fact that rents were crushing—when paid in kind they were as high as 40–50 per cent of the crop. A drastic land reform was carried out by the Viet Minh but this was to prove of brief duration for, once he had consolidated his power, Ngo Dinh Diem, with American backing, pushed through his own 'land reform'. Through the various concessions it made to the landlord group (one of the mainstays of the Diem régime) it was possible, even after the reform, for a landlord to hold a hundred times as much land as a peasant; moreover, whereas the Viet Minh reform had confiscated the land and given it to the peasant, under the Diem reform the landlord was generously compensated for all land redistributed. The Diem reform, in fact, seemed in the eyes of the peasant a long step backwards; he was being sold land the Viet Minh had given him or was told the Government was reducing rents the Viet Minh had abolished. . . . A rising tide of peasant dissatisfaction coincided with increasing criticism of the authoritarian character of the Diem régime in many quarters; this was met by increasing barbarity and repression by police and army and this in turn by increasing armed opposition by the rural masses. By the end of March 1959 South Vietnam was, in the words of Diem himself, 'a nation at war'.

After the withdrawal of the French in 1954 the South Vietnamese political scene was characterised by two features: first, the dominance of Diem and his family, secondly by the progressive replacement of French by American influence. Diem was a fanatical anti-communist and his political outlook filled him admirably to play a major role in the American policy of building up South Vietnam as an anti-communist bastion and an essential element in the United States military policy in Southeast Asia. Heavy American aid and an increasing flow of American advisors enabled him to consolidate his position; this process involved the neutralisation of the various sects which, with their own armies, had constituted a major challenge to the authority of the central government. The consolidation of Diem's position was not, however, followed by any effective policy of social and economic development which would have benefited the peasant masses who made up some nine-tenths of the population and which would have given the régime the measure of broad popular support it needed. Instead, the régime became increasingly repressive and dictatorial in character and power became increasingly concentrated in the hands of Diem and his family; these were Catholics, members of the small and influential Catholic minority in South Vietnam, and their policies served merely to widen yet further the gap between the Catholics of Vietnam and a Buddhist majority which was becoming both conscious of its power and politically articulate. Thus there developed a situation in which the need of the Diem régime to buttress its own position by smashing every type of opposition and the strategic needs of American policy, which demanded that South Vietnam be purged of anything that might remotely serve the communist cause, coincided—and the wave of mounting repression drove large sectors of the population into open and bitter armed resistance to the central government and its American sponsors. Under such conditions any real economic development has been impossible. Diem's own attitudes to economic development had in any case resulted in minimal economic progress even before the civil war reached an acute stage. Rejecting both capitalism and communism he sought to attain 'something similar to the organisational form of co-operatives', aiming at economic progress through direct governmental participation in industry and within the framework of a planned economy. But a planned economy is scarcely possible in a country with an inexperienced and inefficient bureaucracy and without an intelligent development programme and a policy of governmental development of industry could not be expected to achieve any major success given the limited funds available and the imbalance in their allocation. A policy which, between 1955 and 1960, allocated 45 per cent of all American project aid to highway development and only 9 per cent to agriculture could scarcely be expected to achieve any major economic break-through. . . .

The massive inflow of American aid was an additional factor inhibiting real economic growth. This aid has been essential to prop up the country's tottering economy; at the same time, it warped the economic development of the nation. It helped to close the gap between imports and exports (in 1963 imports were four times the value of exports) and provided the great bulk of the budget expenditure (in 1958, the last year for which data was available, the proportion was almost two-thirds). At the same time the aid, much in the shape of American goods, has been directed to the maintenance of the consumption levels of a small group rather than to laying the basis for sound economic growth; the imports of textiles were thus approximately equal to the imports of industrial equipment and machinery, those of cars and pharmaceuticals to the value of the fertilisers so desperately needed by Vietnamese agriculture. And the heavy drain on funds for military purposes (to cope with the insurrection which grew out of the agrarian situation) has meant that the non-military sector of the country's life has been starved.

The elimination of Diem did not basically alter the situation. The deep-seated agrarian problem remained, in spite of token reforms. Industrial development has been negligible. Politico-military attempts to halt the guerrilla war, such as the Staley Plan for resettlement (modelled partly on British policy in Malaya during the Emergency), proved largely ineffective and in the last year or so the situation has come increasingly to resemble that of the country during the final stages of French domination, with the forces of the Government and the United States controlling limited 'bridgeheads' in the cities and parts of the countryside by day and with the guerrilla forces of the National Liberation Front dominating most of rural Vietnam by night. And the very ruthlessness with which Diem eliminated all opposition meant that when he was removed there were no alternative figures around whom an effective government might take shape; the result has been a series of military juntas preoccupied with maintaining themselves in power as long as possible and whose opportunism—and blindness to anything save the military situation—prevented them mobilising any mass support among the people whose interests they claim to serve. These groups, in the eyes of many Southeast Asians, represent merely a puppet régime and provide a façade behind which American forces and American military power are becoming more and more deeply involved in the struggle against the peasant guerrillas of the Liberation Front. Under such circumstances the war appears increasingly as a war waged by the West against a coloured people or as a war of the 'haves' against the 'have-nots'. Such a war threatens to destroy the Western image in Southeast Asia as completely and effectively as the massed aerial bombardments and widespread use of chemical defoliants are shattering Vietnamese society and destroying the country's productive potential for years to come.

(C) The Communist-bloc Countries

To get the communist (or socialist) countries of Southeast and east Asia into correct perspective we must bear in mind, first, that the state control of the economy (usually regarded as typical of socialist countries) reaches far back into the early history of many Asian peoples—as early as the Han Dynasty in China certain industries were government monopolies and the state certainly played an important role in the social and economic spheres in mediaeval Cambodia. Secondly, that socialism of Western (i.e. Marxist) inspiration has a long history in Southeast Asia; it certainly dates back some forty years in the Indochinese lands, for example. Thirdly, that the region shows a wide spectrum of socialisms, ranging from the almost English-style socialism of Singapore through the Buddhist socialisms of Burma and Cambodia to the austere Marxist-Leninist socialism of North Vietnam; the term 'socialist' or even 'communist' is a blanket term which may cover a wide diversity of political forms. Fourthly, and the Sino-Soviet differences and their repercussions in Asia underline this, these Asian socialisms may be significantly different in form and content from the European socialisms. This difference is often overlooked, but it is scarcely possible to understand the contemporary scene or the forces working to change it unless we bear them in mind.

The distinguishing features of the Asian socialist societies are largely rooted in local conditions. They are societies which are starting their economic and social development from a point of departure much lower than that of, say, the U.S.S.R.; they confront the problems posed by much greater densities of population and by a rate of population growth well in excess of those which confronted the emerging socialisms of Europe and, given this lower base and different demographic conditions, they must mobilise their populations much more fully if they are ever to reach the point of self-sustaining economic growth; they are, moreover, peasant societies and, in contrast to the West, where the revolutions were urban-based, the success of *their* revolutions has depended largely on the mass support of the peasantry; finally, since their revolutions are still young, since their societies have not begun to approach the affluence of Soviet society, since they are still 'have-nots' by comparison with the 'haves' of the established European socialist world, they preserve a greater community of interest with the other 'have-nots' of the globe and from this springs a different attitude to 'co-existence' and to 'wars of national liberation'. Under these conditions, the divergences between the countries of the Asian communist bloc and the 'European' communist countries are in some respects larger than those which separate the U.S.S.R. and the U.S.A.; as one French scholar has commented, the Iron Curtain has virtually disappeared in eastern Europe, to re-appear along the Soviet–Chinese frontier. . . .

The Chinese revolution and the reshaping of Chinese society which followed have provided the inspiration for, and the model for, other Asian communist régimes and for left-wing groups in Southeast Asia such as the Pathet Lao or the South Vietnamese Liberation Front. Nevertheless, it is not a model that is servilely copied; the wide diversity of historical and social conditions in Southeast Asia makes such a copying quite unrealistic. Moreover, the strength of local nationalist feeling is an additional force which gives a strong indigenous quality to each of the Asian communist régimes; this is a force which is too often overlooked by the West, which tends to attribute to world communism a monolithic quality which is as unreal as the concept of a monolithic capitalism. It cannot be said with any certainty that North Vietnam has decisively chosen the Chinese or the Soviet camp; it receives aid from and maintains friendly contact with both groups and is striving to build a society 'Vietnamese in form and socialist in content'.

THE DEMOCRATIC REPUBLIC OF NORTH VIETNAM

The Democratic Republic of North Vietnam came into existence after a savage and protracted 'war of national liberation' waged against the French colonial régime. This war was terminated by the Geneva Agreements of 1954; these, as we have already seen, provided for what was to be a temporary division of the Vietnamese lands along the line of the 17th parallel. The Geneva Agreements provided for elections, which might have restored the unity of Vietnam, in 1956; these, however, were never held and the 17th parallel became one of the most absolute barriers in the world, a barrier along which the American-supported South Vietnamese régime abutted on the communist bloc, a barrier which cut off a food-deficit, mineral-rich North from a food-surplus, mineral-deficient South.

The new state was born from the struggles and the dedication of a peasant army, of the Vietnamese masses, led by Ho Chi Minh and Vo Nguyen Giap. It emerged in the same fashion as the Chinese People's Republic and, like the Chinese People's Republic, it emerged as a communist state. And, like China, it faced major problems of economic and social reconstruction. It was cut off by a new and impermeable frontier from its traditional source of rice—the South; the countryside had been devastated by years of war and by the 'scorched earth' policy of the French; its transport system had been largely destroyed; such limited industry as had been established during the colonial régime was reduced to rubble. Under these conditions it survived only as a result of food grains sent by the U.S.S.R. and China; the eventual consolidation of the régime would have been impossible had it failed to win 'the battle for rice'.

As in China, the breakthrough on the food front was achieved by the massive mobilisation of the peasantry which absorbed the unemployment and underemployment which had been endemic in the crowded countryside of the Red River lowland and converted it into a factor for progress. Working with their hoes and their pannier baskets they dug thousands of kilometres of canals, reconstructed and extended the network of dykes and barrages so that by 1959 a total of two million hectares were under irrigation, and transformed some half a million acres of rice-land from single-crop land to land capable of bearing two or three crops a year. By 1955 the production levels of 1939 had been regained; for the next five years a rate of growth of over 10 per cent per annum (possibly exaggerated) was claimed. René Dumont, reporting on his visit to North Vietnam in 1965, stated that rice yields had risen from the pre-war figure of 13·5 quintals per hectare to 20 quintals; he estimated the rate of increase in agricultural production at 3 per cent per annum, noting that, though this is one of the highest growth-rates achieved in any developing country, it is still below the rate of population growth (3·6 per cent per annum).

To a considerable extent the low productivity of agriculture had been due to institutional forces such as feudal survivals in the countryside and the economic policies of the colonial power; these institutional barriers impeded an attack on the physical problems such as flood or drought which contributed to the poverty and precariousness of peasant life. The complete restructuring of rural life carried through by the various agrarian reforms was therefore of decisive importance in the expansion of agricultural production for it liberated the peasant from the old types of exploitation and gave the land to the tiller. Yet, though the abolition of the old system meant that the 625,000 tons of grain which had formerly gone as rent to the landlords now swelled the peasants' larder, problems remained. Of these, the most important was the small size of the peasant's holding—averaging 1,200 square metres (See Plate 13)—and its fragmentation. The development of 'semi-socialist' co-operatives, pooling land, work animals and implements, went far towards solving this problem; virtually the entire peasant population is now organised in co-operatives, one-third of which are fully socialist. There has been no evidence that the North Vietnamese, who followed the Chinese model in their earlier agrarian reforms, are following the Chinese model in the organisation of much larger units, the people's communes. They have, however, begun to diversify the cropping pattern by expanding the production of industrial crops and livestock and to push ahead with the agricultural development of the higher land around the margins of the Red River lowland. The agricultural economy remains none the less a precarious economy: precarious because of the difficulties of matching population expansion with increases in food output, precarious also because the whole agricultural economy of the lowland is dependent upon an elaborate system of dyking and drainage and this is increasingly dependent on a limited number of pumping stations and electric generating plants which are highly vulnerable to military attack from the air.

The agricultural economy is integrated into a planned economy on socialist lines. Economic planning has passed through three stages; the first, from 1954 to 1957, was the period of reconstruction which involved rebuilding the war-ravaged infrastructure of the economy; the second, from 1958 to 1960, was a transitional period; the third, which began in 1961, is the period of the First Five Year Plan. The basic aims of the Plan are twofold: to develop agriculture and to establish the heavy industrial base which alone will make possible the modernisation of the whole economy. The North has considerable assets for such an industrial development; anthracite, iron ore, tin, chrome and other metals make it the obvious heavy industrial base for all of the Indochinese lands. Nevertheless, it faced major difficulties, above all, the limited size of the industrial labour force (only 16 per cent of the labour force engaged in handicrafts and modern industry were in the modern industrial sector), and the absence of cadres and trained technicians (at the end of 1955 the country possessed only twenty-three trained engineers). These bottle-necks have been largely overcome and with limited technical and economic aid from the other countries of the communist bloc there has been a slow but steady elaboration of a modern industrial sector; in part this is localised around Hanoi but the dangers of excessive concentration have been avoided: there has been dispersion of industry into pre-existing cities (e.g. Haiphong) as well as the creation of new industrial centres such as the textile and light industrial centre of Nam Dinh and the new town which has grown up around the Thai Nguyen iron and steel plant. The development of this industrial sector is a major achievement for a poverty-stricken country such as North Vietnam and it has no parallel elsewhere in Southeast Asia. As in China the achievement has been possible only because of the massive mobilisation of labour the régime has carried out, and the dedication and self-imposed austerity of the leaders and the masses. It is a tragedy, not only for North Vietnam but also for the Indo-chinese lands as a whole that this emerging industrial zone, laboriously built up over ten years of uphill struggle, is systematically being wiped out by the massed attacks of American bombers.

The achievements of the North Vietnamese in the economic field have been considerable and they demonstrate to the rest of Southeast Asia the conditions under which real economic progress is possible. The achievements in the socio-cultural field, more specifically in the field of minority policy, have been equally striking and these, in the long run, may prove of even greater relevance to the neighbouring countries of Southeast Asia. As in many other countries of this region two worlds come into contact—the world of the majority people, in this case the Vietnamese, and the world, or the many small worlds, of the minority peoples. The Vietnamese occupy solidly the Red River lowland; the fringing uplands contain some fifty to sixty different tribal groups. Many of these have languages, histories and social systems quite different to those of the Vietnamese and to weld them into a unified state without destroying their individuality poses major problems. The North Vietnamese minority policy follows closely that of China; it provides for the full development of these peoples and recognises their individuality by granting a considerable measure of administrative autonomy to the larger and more compact groups. An essential element in the minority policy is the School for National Minorities in Hanoi; here research into the history and problems of these groups is carried on, new scripts developed for those groups with no written languages and cadres specialising in various fields—health, education, agriculture—are trained before returning to work among their own people. Such a policy makes it possible to build a strong and unified state out of widely disparate elements and has an obvious relevance to other Southeast Asian states who face the same problem of social and cultural diversity and of integrating formerly despised and backward minority peoples into a political and economic structure dominated by a more advanced majority group.

CHAPTER 10

The Contours of the Future

IT IS appropriate, in conclusion, to draw together some of the major lineaments of this complex world of Southeast Asia and to attempt to sketch in some of the contours of the future in the region. This latter is not easy, since these lands are going through a stormy period of transition; they are still, figuratively speaking, in the half-light of dawn and it is a dawn darkly shadowed by open war, by civil war and by undeclared war.

The area, it has been stressed, is one of considerable geographical diversity. It is inhabited by a great variety of human groups, at widely contrasting cultural levels, and these are appraising, are developing, an environment which is highly differentiated in physical and biological terms. These Southeast Asian peoples have been exposed to widely differing colonial influences and have emerged as independent nations with widely differing political systems, many of which are still in a state of experimentation and change. Moreover, like small nations all over the world, they have been drawn into, or affected to varying degrees by, the global strategies of the two great power blocs. And, alongside these factors of diversity, there are strong elements of unity. All the countries of Southeast Asia are impoverished by comparison with the countries of the West and of the European Soviet bloc and this impoverishment is increasing in relative terms. The poverty is due to the warping of their economic structures during the colonial period; more specifically, it was due to 'the intrusion of capitalism into a society within which a minority, indigenous or foreign, took advantage of the crippling of indigenous society to confer upon itself exorbitant political, economic and social powers'; the depredations of this group are a major factor limiting the development of an internal market, impeding modernisation, and prolonging the dependence of the economy on foreign markets. Under such conditions the economies (with the exception of North Vietnam) remain heavily agrarian in their emphasis; underemployment in the rural areas is a direct outcome of lack of modernisation and of change in the economic and social structure; a rapid expansion of population aggravates an already difficult situation. These are the conditions facing most Southeast Asian countries and being confronted with uneven effectiveness by their governments; it is out of these conditions that the future political and social geography of the region will grow. . . .

In their drive towards a better life (which means for most of these peoples not only 'to have more' but 'to *be* more') two alternative roads are open to them, the liberal or free enterprise road and the socialist road. The first of these is the road being followed by most of the emerging nations. This is partly because the free enterprise system was the economic system bequeathed by the former colonial power, partly because it is the system that best serves the interests of the governing *élite*, and partly because, in dispensing aid, the United States tends to favour countries whose régimes support free enterprise—and the United States is the greatest donor of aid and without aid the economies and governments of many of the emergent states would crumple. The free enterprise system may be able to achieve a modest rate of economic growth in some emergent countries but has signally failed in many countries. And where it seems to have achieved some measure of success this is often more apparent than real; what at first sight seems an impressive economic advance may, on closer inspection, be due largely to the rapid expansion of export-oriented 'enclave economies', an expansion which conceals the stagnation of the countryside as a whole. In Southeast Asia both Malaya and Thailand illustrate this uneven development, this widening margin between the prospering 'poles of development' (such as the west coast of Malaya or the Bangkok region in Thailand) and the stagnation of large sectors of the back-country. Given the preoccupation of the system with profits this could hardly be otherwise; investment, and especially overseas investment, flows inevitably to those sectors of the economy and to those regions which offer the prospects of the highest and most certain return on investment; there is little prospect of it flowing towards the peasant sector which accounts for some four-fifths of the employment. Just as, on a global scale, the free enterprise system contributes to the widening gap between the affluent nations and the 'have-not' nations, so, too, at the national level does it contribute to the widening of the gap between the *élite* and the masses, between the restricted areas where modern and diversified economies have been built up and the remainder of the country which remains stagnant economically and little touched by modernisation. And in these economic inequalities, which become increasingly glaring with the passage of time, we may find the major cause of the social and political ferment which is involving many of the under-developed countries.

The limited success of the free enterprise system (or of capitalism) is not hard to understand; it arises from the fact that many of the conditions which contributed to the success of the system in the Atlantic world are lacking elsewhere. The class of entrepreneurs, of businessmen, who played a major role in creating the economic structures of Western Europe and North America has no counterpart in Southeast Asia[1] or other parts of the Third World. The abstention from spending, the investment in long-term development projects, which provided the momentum for the industrialisation of the West in the eighteenth and nineteenth centuries, are largely lacking in an area such as Southeast Asia, where investment in land or in commerce offers more immediate and more lucrative returns than investment in secondary industry. And in countries where the large land-owner is still a powerful force the social structure is a major limiting factor to real development; high rents leave the peasant impoverished and thus severely reduce the purchasing power of the great mass of the population while the wealth thus diverted from the peasantry is channeled into either luxury spending by the land-owning group or into the accumulation of yet more land. . . . As the history of Western

[1] The Chinese of Southeast Asia are possibly an exception to this generalisation.

Europe illustrates, agrarian reform is an essential prerequisite for successful industrialisation—and, as the example of South Vietnam today shows, the possibilities of implementing a *real* agrarian reform are limited in some of the Western-aligned countries. The situation is different in North Vietnam which carried out a drastic land reform in the early years of the communist régime; in Cambodia the favourable man/land ratio and the limited extent of tenant farming means that the agrarian problem is not of major importance.

The socialist path has been chosen by North Vietnam, and, in the form of a 'Buddhist socialism', by Burma and Cambodia. It involves the establishment of an overall plan for the national economy; such a plan makes it possible to allocate scarce resources, such as skilled man-power, capital or equipment, to those economic sectors where the need is greatest. Concerned with the development of the country's economy in the interests of the people as a whole rather than with maximising profits, it can achieve a more balanced distribution of development than under the system of economic liberalism; above all, it can bring about a narrowing of the gap between various classes, or between the developed regions of the State territory and the backward regions. It demands a programme which will arouse the enthusiasm of the masses and this may necessitate a restructuring of society through agricultural reform and the active involvement of the people, through the medium of state-controlled enterprise, in the non-agricultural sectors of the economy. And, given this enthusiasm, it is perhaps the only system which can mobilise the greatest hidden wealth of the region—its underemployed or unemployed masses; by so doing, it converts what had been a problem, in the shape of heavy population pressure, into a factor for progress. And while it calls for discipline and austerity, i.e. for the control of consumption so that the resources necessary for the diversification of the economy can be slowly built up, such discipline and austerity have been shown to be essential if an 'underdeveloped' region such as Southeast Asia is to move to the point of self-sustaining economic growth. A French expert has referred to the 'illusion of foreign aid', by which he means the widespread but erroneous belief that large injections of foreign aid can initiate real economic development. Few areas illustrate the truth of his verdict as clearly as Southeast Asia; within Southeast Asia a comparison of, say, South Vietnam which has received hundreds of millions of dollars of aid (or Laos, where the aid *per capita* was among the highest in the world) with North Vietnam, where ten years of uphill struggle, and limited aid from the Sino-Soviet bloc, have created the beginnings of a modern and diversified economy, puts this truth into even clearer focus.

Looking to the future, the trend towards more radical types of political and economic structure may be expected to continue. This will not be because of propaganda or subversion but because the 'liberal'—or free-enterprise—alternative not only fails to 'deliver the goods' in a Third World context but also because it fails to create a decent society; in other words, it not only fails to create the conditions in which men may *have* more but also the conditions in which they may *be* more. This prospect of a leftward shift is one which many in the West regard with fear and suspicion; indeed, at the moment a bloody and ruinous war is being fought to arrest this trend in South Vietnam. Yet even a perfunctory—but objective—examination of conditions in Southeast Asia, in other parts of the Third World, will drive home the fact that for these countries *there is no other solution* to the gigantic problems that face them, that, for the peoples of Southeast Asia, the examples of China, of North Vietnam and above all North Korea provide an object lesson whose significance is becoming increasingly obvious—and relevant. If this is true, then many of the existing Southeast Asian régimes may prove to be transitional phenomena, whose continuing existence is made possible only by massive external support which maintains the régimes in power without at the same time solving the economic problems which beset them. And with mounting population pressure these problems grow inexorably more acute.

The comments above are not meant to imply, as some Western politicians appear to believe, that the whole of this region faces the prospect of integration or absorption into a monolithic communist bloc. The strength of local nationalisms—well illustrated by Cambodia or Vietnam—is likely to

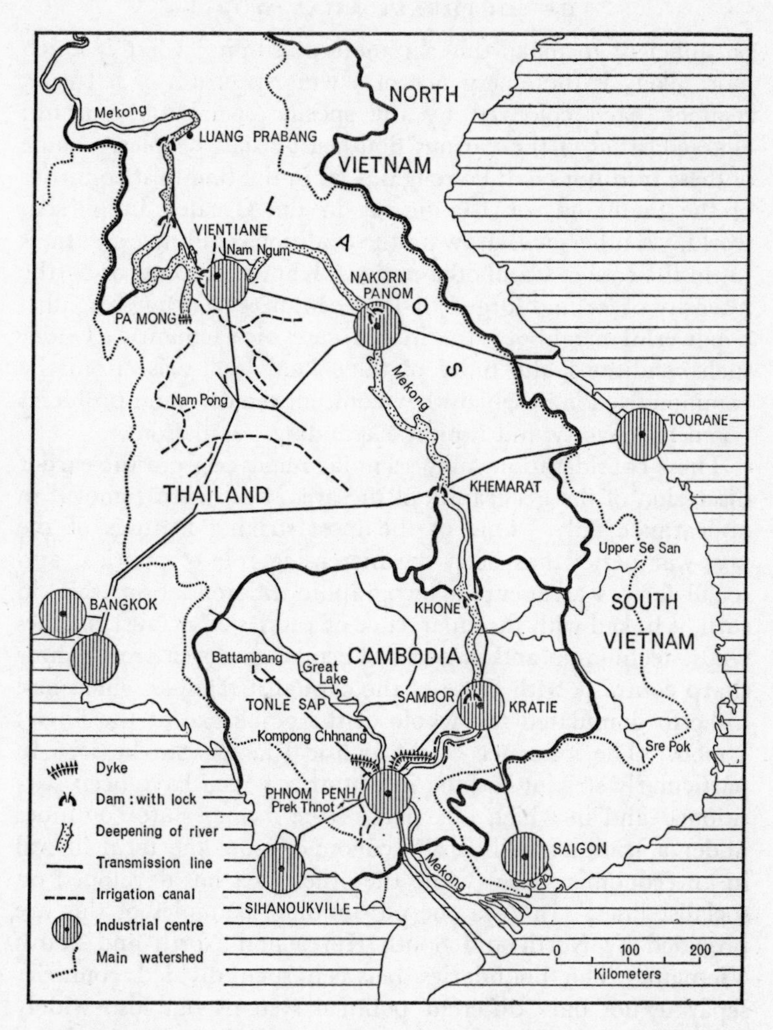

28 The Mekong Project. An example of a (largely Western-conceived) project of multi-purpose development integrating irrigation, flood control and electricity generation. A scheme which may take decades to materialise and is dependent on political stability in the region and large-scale outside aid. Whether a large-scale project of this type, which carries with it the danger that it will create merely a series of 'islands' of development, leaving the back country untouched, is preferable to a wide proliferation of small water-control and power generating projects on the Chinese pattern is something Southeast Asians will have themselves to decide.

be sufficient to make this a remote possibility; what *is* much more likely is the emergence of a wide spectrum of left-wing régimes, each coloured by the specific social and cultural characteristics of the various Southeast Asian peoples. Some of these traditions will be religious, as in the Buddhist countries of the mainland, or Islamic, as in the Greater Indonesian world; yet others will draw on the traditions of former greatness (as in the case of Cambodia and the Khmer Empire) or on the intensity of feelings forged by long centuries of struggle against a powerful neighbour (as in the case of Vietnam). Under such conditions, the unity of these lands will arise from the common fashion in which they confront the common problems posed by poverty and rapidly expanding populations.

These considerations may seem far removed from the earlier discussion of the geography of the area, but it is a removal in appearance only. One of the most striking features of the post-war period has been the increasing role of political and social factors as agents of geographic differentiation; this, in turn, is linked with the emergence of a series of socialist régimes whose techniques and patterns of economic development show sharp contrasts with those of the capitalist régimes which had hitherto dominated the whole of the globe except the Soviet Union. The influence of the political factor can be seen in particularly striking fashion in countries which have been partitioned and in which one part of the former state continues under a traditional 'liberal' economy (using the term liberal in an economic sense) while the other part has developed on socialist lines. In Asia the outstanding examples of this are provided by North and South Korea and North and South Vietnam. The boundaries between such divided countries separate not only different political systems but also widely differing social and economic systems and, since the social and economic system plays a major role in shaping the geography of a country, these boundaries now separate regions with sharply contrasting geographies. Thus, among the impressions on the cultural landscape of a socialist system are the beginning of territory-wide modernisation and diversification of the economy; the development of a series of dispersed industrial complexes; urban growth on a controlled rather than *laissez-faire* basis; the reshaping of the social and economic structure of the rural areas through agrarian reform, a reshaping which, by releasing 'hidden resources' of labour, makes possible the physical transformation of the countryside through irrigation development; finally, the attempts to integrate fully into the country's life minority groups who had formerly been relegated to the category of second-grade citizens. Such developments stand in sharp contrast to the widening gap in levels of modernisation and standards of life which separates the 'poles of development' in non-socialist societies from the stagnating back country.

The hesitant but increasingly inevitable penetration of the Southeast Asian world by socialist concepts of planning and development will, in the years ahead, result in a geography very different from the contemporary geography of Southeast Asia. Part of the inspiration for the ideas which shape this new world will be derived from the ancient and luminous cultures of the area, part from the lessons drawn from the experience of the other Asian socialist states. In this process of development many of the glaring contrasts in levels of living and economic opportunity (between classes or between areas) will be progressively eliminated in Southeast Asia and, what is even more important, the rise of modern and diversified economies will make it possible for the peoples of the region to begin, first to arrest, then to narrow, the widening economic differential between themselves and the affluent nations of the Atlantic world.

THE NATIONS OF SOUTHEAST ASIA

STATISTICAL SUMMARY

	Cambodia	*Union of Burma*	*Indonesia*	*Philippines*
Area (square kilometres)	172,511	678,033	1,491,564	299,681
Population:				
Total	5·6 million	22·3 million	94·25 million	27·4 million
Density per square kilometre	32	33	63	90
Growth rate (per annum)	3·2	1·9	2·1	3·1
% Population 14 years or less	44·7	41·3	42·1	45·7
Ethnic groups (%)	Khmers 83, tribal peoples 7, others 10	Burmese 68, Shan 8·7, Karen 7·7, others 15·6	Indonesian 97, Chinese 2·7	Tagalog 21·02, Cebuano 24·10, Iloco 12, others 54·9
% Urban dwelling	13·0	9·6	11·7	9·1
Cultivated Area:				
Total (million hectares)	2·35	8·6	17·68	6·78
Major crops (production)	Rice 2·6 M tons	Rice 8·0 M tons	Rice 12·5 M tons, Rubber 217,000 tons	Rice 3·9 M tons
Livestock (000s):				
Pigs	616	652	1,880	6,190
Buffaloes	440	1,005	2,860	3,450
Cattle	1,250	5,250	4,950	1,050
Mineral production (tons)		Crude petroleum 584,000, tin concentrates 900	Petroleum 22·7 M, Tin 1,466, Natural Gas 3,492 M m³	Petroleum 244,000, Iron ore 116,000
Electricity production	79 M kwh	512 M kwh	1,980 M kwh	3,680 M kwh
Industrial production	Cement 50,000 tons	Cement 120,000 tons, Cotton yarn 11 M lb.	Cotton textiles 64 M metres	Cotton fabrics 140 M metres
G.N.P. per capita ($)	155	121	148	282
Composition of export trade	Rubber 40·1, Rice 33·3, maize 11·9	Rice 66·3, Timber 8·7, Oil-seeds 5·2	Rubber 45·0, Petroleum and products 16·3	Copra 26·1, Sugar 22·8, Timber 15·2

	Thailand	Laos	Vietnam	North Vietnam	(and Singapore)
Area (square kilometres)	514,000	236,800	170,806	159,000	332,215
Population:					
Total	26·4 million	1·8 million	14·1 million	16·4 million	10·18 million
Density per square kilometre	51	8	83	106	30·5
Growth rate (per annum)	3·1	3·2	2·2[1]	3·6[3]	2·76
% Population 14 years or less	43·2	(40·8)	36·6[1]	36·6[1]	45·6
Ethnic groups (%)	Thai 88, Chinese 9, Muslim Malays 3	Lao almost one-half, Tribal Thai 15, others 35	Vietnamese 81·3, hill tribes 7·7, others 11	Vietnames 92, Thai 5·6, hill tribes 2	Malay 39·2, other Malaysian 7, Chinese 42·2, others 11·6
% Urban dwelling	9·1	3	10·8[2]	3·1	
Cultivated Area:					
Total (million hectares)	10·08	1	2·9	2·0[3]	5·5
Major crops (production)	Rice 10 M tons, Jute 350,000 tons, Rubber 193,000	Rice 0·52 M tons	Rice 4·61 M tons, Rubber 75,000 tons	Rice 4·66 M tons	Rice 1·0 M tons Rubber 830,000 tons
Livestock (000s):					
Pigs	5,250	n.a.	3,130	1943	1,269
Buffaloes	6,750	440	754	2,822	352
Cattle	5,100	190	889	4,876	334
Mineral production (tons)	Iron ore 190,000, Tin ore 21,600	—	Coal 71,000	Coal 2·8 M	Tin concentrates 60,000
Electricity production	775 M kwh	0·78 M kwh	359 M kwh	276 M kwh	2,323 M kw
Industrial production	Cement 1·06 M tons	—	Cement 73,000 tons, Cotton and Rayon fabrics 182 M m	Cement 453,000 tons, Textiles 90 M metres	Cement 360,000 tons
G.N.P. per capita ($)	202	104	210	n.a.	261
Composition of export trade	Rice 30·5, Rubber 30·4, Maize 6·5	Tin ore 46·3	Rubber 56·1, Rice 32·1		Rubber 53·5, tin (metal and concentrates) 15·6
Political orientation	pro-Western	Divided by civil war	Divided by civil war	Communist	pro-Western

Notes: [1] North and South Vietnam. [2] Cities of 100,000 and over. [3] Dumont *La Chine surpeuplée* (Paris, 1965).

SELECTED BIBLIOGRAPHY

(*Paperbacks are indicated by an asterisk*)

PERSPECTIVES

Fanon, F., *The Damned.* Fundamental to an understanding of the attitudes and aspirations of those nations which have emerged from colonial status and which are endeavouring to create a decent society and a modern economy. (Paris 1963)

Heilbroner, R. L., *The Future as History* (New York 1959)

Heilbroner, R. L., *The Great Ascent.* Heilbroner's two studies are perhaps the best introduction (in English) to the social, economic and political problems facing regions such as Southeast Asia. (New York 1963)

Moussa, P., *The Underprivileged Nations.* A Western view of the problems of the 'proletarian nations'. (London 1962)

Worsley, P., 'Imperial Retreat' in *Out of Apathy*, ed. E. P. Thompson (London 1960)

Worsley, P., *The Third World.* The problems posed by the political, social and economic emergence of two-thirds of mankind as seen by one of Britain's leading sociologists. (London 1964)

GENERAL HISTORICAL AND POLITICAL

*Butwell, R., *Southeast Asia: Today and Tomorrow* (New York 1961)

Clubb, O. E., *The United States and the Sino-Soviet Bloc in Southeast Asia* (Washington 1962)

Cowan, C. D. (Editor), *The Economic Development of South-East Asia* (London 1964)

*Edwardes, M., *Asia in the Balance.* Possibly the best short introduction to the political and economic problems of modern Asia. (Harmondsworth 1962)

Edwardes, M., *Asia in the European Age* (London 1961)

Douglas, W. O., *North From Malaya.* An American liberal's impressions of Southeast Asia during the sunset of colonialism. (London 1954)

*Fifield, R. H., *Southeast Asia in United States Policy* (New York, London 1963)

Hall, D. G. E., *A History of Southeast Asia* (London 1955)

*Harris, R., *Independence and After*. An excellent short account of the social and economic revolutions taking place in Southeast Asia with special emphasis on the Indochinese lands. (O.U.P., London 1962)

Harrison, B., *South-East Asia: A Short History* (London 1963)

Kahin, G. McT. (Editor), *Governments and Politics of Southeast Asia*. Studies of six of the Southeast Asian countries by leading U.S. experts. (Cornell, New York 1959)

Kennedy, D. E., *The Security of Southern Asia*. A detailed and balanced analysis of the strategic situation in Southeast Asia and of the significance of China. (Institute of Strategic Studies, London 1965)

Panikkar, K. M., *Asia and Western Dominance*. A fundamental book by the greatest Asian historian, looking at Asian history through Asian eyes. (London 1953)

Pelzer, K., *Pioneer Settlement in the Asiatic Tropics*. The essential background to any study of land use and rural problems in Southeast Asia. (New York 1945)

Purcell, V., *The Revolution in Southeast Asia*. A balanced account of the process of transition from colonial status to independence and of the aspirations of Southeast Asia's peoples. (London 1962)

White, G. F. and others, *Economic and Social Aspects of Lower Mekong Development* (1962—no publisher given)

GENERAL SOCIAL AND CULTURAL GEOGRAPHY

Burling, R., *Hill Farms and Padi Fields: Life in Mainland Southeast Asia*. Useful introduction, from anthropological viewpoint, to some aspects of Southeast Asia's traditional agricultural systems. (Englewood Cliffs 1965)

de Bary, W. T. and Embree, A. T., *Approaches to Asian Civilizations*. Various facets of the major Asian civilisations, seen in the light of an Asian Studies programme which integrates the historical and topical methods of approach. (New York 1964)

Du Bois, Cora, *Social Forces in Southeast Asia* (Cambridge, Mass., 1959)

Fisher, C. A., *Southeast Asia*. Likely to remain the fundamental reference work on the area for many years. (London 1964)

Fitzgerald, C. P., *The Third China*. Valuable short account of the Chinese of Southeast Asia. (Sydney 1965)

Hall, D. G. E. (Introduction), *Atlas of Southeast Asia*. A basic reference work for all interested in Southeast Asia, with a useful general account of the area to round off the purely cartographic content. (London, New York 1964)

Jacoby, E. H., *Agrarian Unrest in Southeast Asia*. Discusses some of the rural issues which provide a powerful motive force behind movements for political change in the area. (London 1961)

*Le Thành Khoi, *Histoire de l'Asia du Sud-est* (Paris 1959)

*Matthew, Helen G. (Editor), *Asia in the Modern World*. The past history and culture of the Asian countries and the revolutionary changes transforming them. (New York 1963)

Mende, T., *Southeast Asia between Two Worlds*. Includes India and Pakistan in his definition of Southeast Asia: nevertheless, one of the best analyses of the problems of Southeast and South Asia. (London 1955)

Percheron, M., *Buddha and Buddhism* (London—no date)

Robequain, C. (trans. E. D. Laborde), *Malaya, Indonesia, Borneo and the Philippines*. A cumbersome title for the original volume which appeared in French as *The Malay World*. (London 1954)

Sauer, C., *Agricultural Origins and Dispersals*. (New York 1952)

Spencer, J. E., *Asia East by South*. The best introduction, from the pen of an articulate specialist in Asian matters, to the geography of Asia's eastern and southern fringes. (New York, London 1961)

Spencer, J. E., 'Migration of Rice from Mainland Southeast Asia into Indonesia' in Barrau, J. (Editor), *Plants and the Migrations of Pacific Peoples* (Honolulu 1963)

Thompson, Virginia and Adloff, R., *Minority Problems in Southeast Asia*. Useful account of the indigenous and immigrant minority peoples whose integration poses a major challenge to the countries of the region. (Stanford 1955)

United Nations, *The Asian Population Conference, 1963*. Invaluable symposium of papers analysing the present demographic situation and the problems the region faces in the face of an expanding population. (New York 1964)

Zürcher, E., *Buddhism* ('its origin and spread in words, maps and pictures') (New York 1962)

INDO-CHINA: GENERAL

Chaffard, G., *Indochine: dix ans d'independance*. A valuable and impartial account of the last decade in the Indochinese lands by one of the leading French experts on the region. (Paris 1964)

Gourou, P., *Land Utilisation in Indochina*. Remains a fundamental work for all who wish to understand the patterns and problems of rural life in Indochina. (New York 1945)

Lewis, N., *A Dragon Apparent* (sub-titled 'Travels in Indo-China') (London 1951)

Nuttonson, M. Y., *The Physical Environment and Agriculture of Vietnam, Laos and Cambodia* (Washington 1963)

VIETNAM

Brodrick, A. H., *Little China: The Annamese Lands* (London 1942)

Chesneaux, J., *Le Viet-nam*. Perhaps the best general account of Vietnam with a particularly valuable analysis of the 'warping' of the economy during the French period. (Paris 1955)

China Quarterly, Number 9, Special issue on North Vietnam (London 1962)

Gettleman, M. E. (Editor), *Vietnam: History, Documents and Opinions on a Major World Crisis.* A well-balanced collection of excerpts covering various aspects of Vietnamese life from the pre-colonial period to the escalation of the Second Indochinese War. (Greenwich, Conn., 1965, Harmondsworth 1966)

Lacouture, J., *Le Vietnam entre deux paix* (Paris 1965)

Murti, B. S. N., *Vietnam Divided: The Unfinished Struggle.* A full analysis of the complexities of the Vietnamese situation by a former Indian member of the International Control Commission. (London 1964)

Mus, P., *Vietnam: Sociologie d'une guerre.* The best account of the quality—and the strengths—of Vietnamese rural life. (Paris 1952)

Nguyen, Kien, *Le sud-vietnam depuis Dien-Bien-Phu.* A closely documented and critical analysis, from a left-wing viewpoint, of the processes whereby the United States replaced France in Vietnam and of the roots of the present conflict. (Paris 1963)

Raskin, M. G. and Fall, B. *The Viet-Nam Reader* (New York 1965). Provides much of the basic documentation needed to understand the current conflict in Vietnam, its consequences and the alternatives to present U.S. policy.

CAMBODIA

Brodrick, A. H., *Little Vehicle: Cambodia and Laos* (London—no date)

Delvert, J., *Le paysan cambodgien.* Meticulous and detailed account of Cambodian peasant life, with valuable maps and photographs. (Paris, La Haye 1961)

Migot, A., *Les Khmers.* History of the Khmer people from earliest times. A sympathetic and sensitive appraisal by a French doctor who has lived and worked in Cambodia and other Asian countries. (Paris 1960)

Steinberg, D. J., *Cambodia* (New Haven 1959).

*Thierry, Solange, *Les Khmers.* The best short introduction (with carefully-chosen and striking illustrations) to the Khmer people and their land, written by a perceptive observer who succeeds in capturing in words the poetry and gentle beauty of the country and its people. (Paris 1964)

INDONESIA

Geertz, C., *Agricultural Involution: The Processes of Ecological Change in Indonesia.* Basic contrasts in the 'cultural ecology' of Indonesia and the crystallisation of the pattern in classical and colonial times. (Berkeley and Los Angeles 1963)

Kennedy, R., *The Ageless Indies.* (New York 1942)

Mackie, J. A. C., 'The Indonesian Economy, 1950–63' in *Studien zur Entwicklung in Süd- und Ostasien* (Neue Folge, Teil 3: Indonesien) (Frankfurt, Berlin 1964)

McVey, Ruth T. (Editor), *Indonesia.* Ten essays by leading authorities in their field on various aspects of contemporary Indonesia. (New Haven 1963)

PHILIPPINES

Golay, F. H., *The Philippines: Public Policy and National Economic Development* (Cornell, New York 1961)

Spencer, J. E., *Land and People in the Philippines.* The basic text on the geography of the islands; a wealth of meticulous detail which never obscures the broad patterns of landscape and people and which is infused with a historical and sociological awareness rare in geographic writing. (Berkeley 1952)

LAOS

Le Bar, F. M. and Suddard, A., *Laos.* A useful attempt to give a picture of a country for which even such basic statistics as population totals are either suspect or completely lacking and which has scarcely emerged as a nation in any meaningful sense of the term. (New Haven 1960)

THAILAND

Pendleton, R. L., *Thailand.* The basic text—yet inexplicably thin on the texture of Thai life or the problems which face the Thai state. (New York 1962)

BURMA

Leach, E., 'The Political Future of Burma' in *Futuribles*, ed. B. de Jouvenel. A first-rate short study, containing in its thirty-two pages more information and more penetrating observations on Burmese problems than many books ten times the length. (Geneva 1963)

Lewis, N., *Golden Earth* (Burma). The landscape, peoples, and problems of emergent Burma captured in an evocative prose by one of the outstanding travel writers of our time. (London 1952)

Tinker, Hugh, *The Union of Burma* (London 1957)

MALAYA AND SINGAPORE

*Ho, R., *Environment, Man and Development in Malaya.* The problems and potentials of Malaya analysed by one of Malaya's leading geographers. (Kuala Lumpur 1962)

International Bank for Reconstruction and Development, *Report on the Economic Aspects of Malaysia.* Invaluable for its statistical documentation of the economy and role of the component units of Malaysia. (Kuala Lumpur 1963)

Kirkup, J., *Tropic Temper.* A perceptive and unusual account of Malaya and Malayan life based on the year the author spent as Visiting Professor at the University of Malaya in Kuala Lumpur. (London 1963)

McKie, R., *Malaysia in Focus* (Sydney 1963)

Ooi, Jin-bee, *Land, People and Economy in Malaya.* A comprehensive geography of the country, providing the background for more detailed and social and political analysis. (London 1963)

Purcell, V., *Malaysia* (London 1965)

Silcock, T. H. (Editor), *Readings in Malayan Economics* (Singapore 1961)

Wang, Gungwu, *Malaysia: A Survey.* Twenty-six major essays on the people, politics and economy of Malaysia. (New York, London 1964)

NOVELS, SHORT STORIES AND POETRY

*Burgess, A., *Malayan Trilogy.* Three novels which capture the quality of Malay life, by a novelist who matches his acuteness of observation with a keen—and often hilarious—sense of humour. (London 1964)

Fabricius, J., *Girdle of Emerald.*

Gonzalez, N. V. M., *Children of the Ash-covered Loam.* Short stories dealing with 'the clash between the city and the farm, the impact of the sophisticate upon the primitive, the collision between reality and the unreal city'. (Manila 1954)

Gonzalez, N. V. M., *The Bamboo Dancers.* 'A record of the days when our people (the Filipinos) nimbly danced to the clash of cultures'. (Manila 1960)

Gonzalez, N. V. M., *Look, Stranger, on this Island Now* (Manila 1963)

Greene, G., *The Quiet American.* South Vietnam and the inability of the Americans, imprisoned within the mental confines of their own culture, to even begin to understand the Vietnamese mentality. (London 1955)

*Han Suyin, *And the Rain my Drink.* Malaya during the Emergency—and the problems of creating a unified state from three so dissimilar groups as Malay, Chinese and Indian. (London 1956)

Han Suyin, *The Four Faces.* 'Truth concealed as fiction', in the shape of a satirical novel set in modern Cambodia. (London 1963)

Hougron, J., *Blaze of the Sun.* This and the two succeeding volumes form the triology 'The Indochinese Night' which deals with the closing stages of French rule in Indochina. (London 1954)

Hougron, J., *The Fugitive* (London 1955)
Hougron, J., *Reap the Whirlwind* (London 1958)
*Hougron, J., *Barbarians Country.* The corruption of the governed and the governing in the last stages of French rule in Indochina. (London 1963)
*Kirkup, J. (Introduction), *Modern Malay Verse* (*Sajak 2 Melayu Baru*). A remarkable anthology of poets whose work throws a flood of light on the forces working to transform Malay society and on the aspirations and fears of the Malay people. (Kuala Lumpur 1963)
*Lederer, W. J. and Burdick, E., *The Ugly American.* A tragic 'comedy of errors' with as its central theme the inability of the Americans to understand, or to come to terms with, either the traditional pattern of Southeast Asian life or the forces working to transform it. (London 1960)
Lubis, Mochtar, *Twilight in Djakarta.* The corruption and disintegration in the capital of emerging Indonesia, features which are typical of the capital cities and political life of many of the new nations caught up in the power struggles of the major political blocs. (London 1963)
Raffel, B. (Editor), *An Anthology of Modern Indonesian Poetry.* An excellent cross-section of Indonesian poetry, the poets ranging from an aristocrat like Amir Hamzar to a guerrilla fighter like Chairil Anwar. (Berkeley and Los Angeles 1964)
Reynolds, J., *A Sort of Beauty* (paperback edition: *Woman of Bangkok*). The sophisticated society of modern Bangkok. (London 1956)
Rizal, J. (trans. Leon Ma Guerrero) *Noli Me Tangere.* The greatest of Filipino novels by the greatest figure in the Filipino nationalist movement. (London 1961)
Wigmore, L., *Span.* An anthology of Asian and Australian writing. (Melbourne 1958)
Wignesan, T., *Bunga Emas: An Anthology of Contemporary Malaysian Literature.* (London 1964)

Index

(Page references to diagrams and maps are marked by † and * respectively: plate references by **)